Lick it

for Juni, Januari and April.
the three most beautiful
people I know.

Lick it

challenge the way you experience food

Marije Vogelzang

BISPUBLISHERS

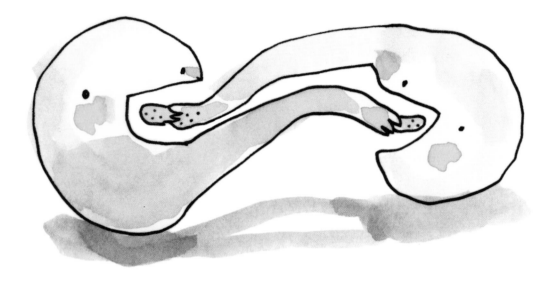

BIS Publishers
Borneostraat 80-A
1094 CP Amsterdam
The Netherlands

t +31 (0)20 515 02 30
bis@bispublishers.com
www.bispublishers.com

ISBN 978-90-636-9650-4
© 2022 Marije Vogelzang and BIS Publishers

preface

I'm not a writer. I'm a designer.

In 1995, as a confused seventeen-year-old with glasses and teased hair (like The Cure's Robert Smith), I started at the Design Academy in Eindhoven, where I was more concerned with going out, drinking and meeting people than designing. I daresay anthropology and philosophy fuelled such interests. I didn't really know what anthropology was at that time, and philosophy seemed to be something captured in Greek marble statues.

I chose to study design because I wanted to do something creative that would also have meaning for other people – in other words, applied design. My early years were bad; so bad I was almost expelled. The academy would have been right to do so because I had no idea what I was doing. I had come from a traditional schooling system where you do what the teacher tells you and are not encouraged to think for yourself. So when I was challenged to come up with something myself and do it of my own accord, I was at a loss. It wasn't until I was on the brink of being kicked out that the penny dropped. I learned to follow my gut instinct, direct myself, research and make things that excited me. From that moment on, everything changed.

I liked owning beautiful objects but not making them. I lacked the patience and love for inanimate materials. 'You can make a table or a cupboard, but you can also choose not to. What does it matter? There's so much stuff already out there,' I thought. I became very enthusiastic about scented objects, transformable materials, matter that could grow and decay and edible products. In short, things that you experience not just with your eyes but with all your senses. Things you can even put into your body! This still feels like pure magic to me.

Once the penny dropped, I started working with organic matter, such as hair, agar-agar and shells. I was terribly nervous before making and presenting my white funeral meal in 1999. (See chapter Death.) Food was not yet considered material for designers: it was for 'chefs – or housewives'. Some fellow students mocked, 'What does a designer do with food?' Yet I felt it was the right thing to do. Food is direct and honest. It may look nice, but it's no use if it doesn't taste good. Food is life, identity, landscape, politics and emotion.

Using food as a material is difficult. You have to deal with its transience, which requires a different attitude to making things with materials that always keep their shape, such as steel, plastic or stone. It also requires a humble attitude, and you cannot force the material to your will like an omnipotent and ruthless God. You can leave a plastic chair for a year, and it will look the same. But you have to keep an eye on food. It has a more significant influence on both the maker's attitude and the world around us. Food is the world's largest economic force. It changes landscapes, cities and digital structures, but it also changes people on the inside. This 'material' penetrates us the most, so it deserves our attention. Put simply: it is our life.

Most designers made useful objects at the middle of the nineties: functionality was key. Then the idea arose, driven by Droog Design, that designers could work more freely. At that time, the Academy (for) Industrial Design Eindhoven changed its name to Design Academy Eindhoven. The school would be about designing itself, whether for industry or just a single piece. I like the German word 'gestaltung', which we translate as 'to design' but literally means 'to give shape to an idea'. Whether that shape is a bronze penis or a brittle biscuit doesn't matter.

The emergence of the idea of conceptual design helped me enormously when, as a third-year student, I made a presentation to my teachers for which I wore a homemade white suit made of too-thick felt – sweating and with hair now trimmed. I had just found out that the mother of my senior teacher, Li Edelkoort, had passed away a few days earlier. I thought I'd made the most misguided work possible as I stood there with my hypothetical funeral meal. I left the tutors to ponder over the white food and hurried out of the room, feeling like a charlatan with my bogus idea. When I returned, the room had a serene atmosphere. Li thanked me warmly. She was visibly moved and told me it had been the perfect experience at the right time. My white funeral meal was subsequently shown at the Design Academy's first presentation at the Salone del Mobile in Milan. It was featured in all kinds of magazines. I didn't know what was happening to me and couldn't believe that you could be successful without having 'traditional design skills'.

In the end, I didn't use food for my graduation project. I didn't dare, because people often told me that food was not a serious subject for designers. I was also afraid of becoming 'the food girl', and I'd never be able to design anything 'real' again. It amuses me now that I'm writing this, but at the time, it was hard to see a future as there was no one else in whose footsteps I could follow. It was unknown what the combination of food and design could mean for the world. Food simply wasn't a subject yet. Despite this, I couldn't resist.

I began with creative catering. Although this was a convenient starting point, the thirty-plus rejections from design agencies I applied to also motivated me. Only Hella Jongerius, where I worked for a year, gave me a role as a junior designer. For seven years, I had two experimental restaurants in Rotterdam and Amsterdam called Proef (which means both 'taste' and 'test' in Dutch). Meanwhile, my design work gathered momentum with exhibitions in cities such as New York, Toronto, Moscow, Shanghai, Cape Town and Tokyo. I travelled the world to give lectures about my work and continued discovering and developing food and design.

It's now twenty-three years later. Various courses and organisations dedicated to Food Design are all over the world, and almost every country has at least several practicing 'food designers'. Food & Design has become a global movement. Nowadays, when you are a designer working with food, you are stepping into a rich tradition. Nevertheless, the profession is still in its infancy. A lot has been done, made and experimented with, but more has not been discovered than has. To this day, there are still people who don't understand why designers get involved with food. When I knew I would be the head of the 'Food Non Food' department – the world's first bachelor's degree in design that focuses on food – at the Design Academy Eindhoven, I had to keep it a secret for a while. At the time, I attended a meeting where someone hypothetically suggested that there might be a department about food one day. A colleague burst into laughter and exclaimed, 'Of course, that will never happen!'

Gestaltung. Giving shape to an idea.
A growing number of people think it's logical that designers work with food. After all, the world faces many challenges regarding food, and innovative ideas are urgently needed. Yet there is a considerable gap between the average person's eating habits and the hard-working, ambitious designer. Many people think that designers are chiefly concerned with making beautiful and functional things, which is not an unusual thought given that this is what designers did in the past. If you consider the description of design as 'giving shape to an idea', then an idea must first be present. Only then can you shape it. In my view, how something looks – its form and aesthetic – is the language with which you communicate your idea. (See chapter Phone eats first.) But what good is language if you have no idea what you want to say with it? Therefore, the essential tool for designers is not the pencil, AutoCAD or saw; it is their capacity for inventive thinking and the mental ability to look at issues from a different angle. Even designers who work purely aesthetically often have a vision, although it may be very personal or intuitive.

But who says inventive thinking is only for designers? I have come across many innovative farmers, creative dieticians, and breathtakingly original chefs as part of my work. Cultivating your creative thinking skills is one of the most fun things to do. You discover that if you give your head more freedom to think differently, you can change the whole world around you. That's why I wrote this book. To challenge you, show you the magic of food, and experience it – despite all the food problems, diets, meat shame and food marketing. If you want to improve your creative thinking skills, you have to do something: with your mouth, your hands, and other people. You will taste differently, smell differently, and assign things a different value. A grape becomes a sex toy. You get more pleasure, see more possibilities, and maybe feel a bit more connected with what's on your plate. After all, you are what you eat.

Really? That tired cliche?
Can't you think of anything else to end this preface with, Marije?

I can, but I won't.
So, just deal with it!

By the way, this is not a science book. It has no footnotes because I'm far too lazy for that sort of thing. If you want to know whether something you read here is correct, just google it.

What I wasn't too lazy for was creating an instagram account where you can see photos of all this book's challenges and the work of the people I interviewed. You can also share your results of the challenges via instagram so that you also contribute to the book yourself. Check out (and tag) **@lickit.book** or send a DM.

Marije Vogelzang

I'll take off my skirts...

foodporn

Do you want to know what's good? Cracking open a warm soft-boiled egg and dipping your finger into the yolk. Watch the egg yolk rise further and further as you push your finger deeper into it. Slowly... a viscous trickle of egg yolk oozes over the edge. The eggshell gets wet. The fluid flows over your other fingers that hold the egg's warm ovoid form. It feels all sticky and warm.

You lift your finger back up and sprinkle some salt on it. Preferably Maldon smoked salt flakes. Then you put your finger into your mouth. The salty yolk stirs your tongue to lick and suck the sticky substance. Your lips close around your finger.

You put your finger in, gently wiggling it back and forth.

Do you know what's also good? Peeling a mandarin (but make sure you ask him softly first). You hear the peel as it rips away from the inner segments. You smell and feel the tiny droplets of essential oil spraying out from the rind. The smell tickles your nose. You slowly undress the clementine. And there it is, a naked, vulnerable ball that you can weigh in your hand. On top is the crown, a beautiful opening. You put your finger in, gently wiggling it back and forth. Tiny drops of juice spill onto your finger. Your finger gets moist as you prise the wedges apart. Then you strip off a segment and listen to how the enclosing membranes relinquish their grip and gently separate. The wedge does not put up a fight and, without protest, reveals what it is hiding: a clutch of droplets individually packed in tiny sacs. You open the wedge and marvel at the spectacle. Once in your mouth, you prod apart the minuscule droplets. The sweet and sour juice flows over your tongue and down your throat.

What I am describing here is something that children sometimes do – until their parents tell them not to play with their food. Or until they must hurry up because swimming lessons are about to start and they can't find their swimming gear.

Explore, look, listen, experience, taste, feel and marvel.
We do this with our bodies when we have the horniest, most sensual sex. The kind where we get completely lost discovering ourselves and the other. The kind where we fall through time. Strangely, children often pay more attention to sensuality than most adults. Many adults earmark sensuality – in the form of sex – for Saturday night. They see sensuality in everyday life as frivolous. And, of course, it's also inefficient.

We eat like we experience porn: quickly, efficiently and until we are full.

Maybe you're the kind of person who dislikes stickiness or licking. 'Ugh, what a mess. Just eat your food!' Still, you can sensually enrich your life by appreciating the shape and smell of food. Perhaps a ripe peach simply feels tender and soft in your hand. Its fragrance might even transport you to balmy summer evenings. For many, luxury dining is the ultimate gastronomic pleasure. But we don't need to make a reservation to indulge our senses. We always have our senses with us. It's not for nothing that #Foodporn is so popular: we eat like we experience porn. We choose what looks good and then eat quickly and efficiently until we are full. It's gratifying, and we certainly enjoy it, but the pleasure can make you numb.

What would you do if I made you a nice horny sandwich with a poached egg, pepper, salt and a knob of butter melting on top? Would you eat it as if eating a sandwich for the first time? Would it be like you've never licked butter off your lips before? Perhaps the salty aftertaste would linger in your mouth as if for the very first time. It might be like being touched for the first time or kissed for the first time. Full of passion.

I spoke about this with food artist Kaye Winwood from Birmingham. She specialises in sensual dining experiences.
'What strikes me most is people say they actually enjoy licking their hand, using their senses, and enjoying food deeply and sensually. The funny thing is that they eat every day but somehow need permission to enjoy food sensuously and explicitly with all their senses. We have the opportunity for a voluptuous experience daily, but few people genuinely embrace pleasure when they eat.'

Kaye also explains that connecting food and sex brings you into the realm of shame. 'We all have senses, a whole-body full. But when we eat, we hardly allow ourselves to surrender to the pleasure and enjoyment. We often dismiss eating as something unimportant. People eat to feed themselves. Sometimes what they eat is a political choice. However, few people eat purely for pleasure. People hold back when they eat.'

Kaye notes that people may experience enjoyment, but there is no question of genuine surrender. 'I want my work to invite people to truly feel that body, which they already have, in a sensual way but then with food. Compare it to mindfulness. When you eat with complete attentiveness, you gain access to pleasure. There are plenty of initiatives that connect food and sex, but they are often vulgar. I'm not interested in eating sushi off each other. As well as sensuality and imagination, my work is simply about pleasure. It's about truly embracing deep-rooted, horny pleasure and about women's emancipation and self-determination. But it's more about allowing pleasure than pleasure itself. Sex and orgasms are still part of the traditional binary culture. I use food to offer a different, sensual language. To make room for a wider interpretation of pleasure.'

Kaye thinks maybe it's a cultural phenomenon that primarily affects women of a certain age. 'However, I have noticed for many women, it is nice to let go of the taboo step by step and surrender to a physical experience that enables them to become very intimate through food. I see my work as a cultural invitation. I create a situation in which the other person can do something themselves. I want the audience of my art to be participants rather than spectators.'

'Children can sometimes truly experience food physically by smelling, licking or listening attentively to the sound of their food. This sensuality in relation to children may sound strange, but it means nothing more than using your senses well. And that's the sensuality I want to explore. I want to embrace childlike wonder and playful discoveries, especially as an adult.'

'A renewed sensual relationship with food could pave the way to a healthier diet.'

Kaye sometimes makes edible perfumes that you can lick. The warmth of your skin fuses with the scent of the fragrance and the wet caress of your tongue. This alone is already an exciting sensation. 'What I find the most interesting is the bridge between what we eat daily and my sensual eating experiences. Why shouldn't we enjoy our food explicitly on a daily basis? Mindful eating can also be exciting. Wouldn't we have a lot more fun? Wouldn't we have more respect for our food and our bodies? We are missing a huge opportunity by not taking advantage of this bridge.' Kaye concludes that it is actually disrespectful to eat without really enjoying it. 'A renewed sensual relationship with food could pave the way to a healthier diet. Eating can help you experience your body more consciously, not only by noticing what it does to you when you eat but also by noticing what it does to you before you eat and allowing that feeling to happen.'

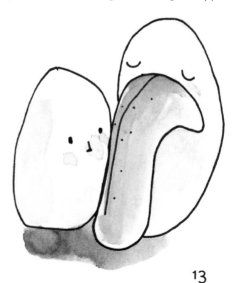

challenge

lick an egg off your hand

I don't know if it's necessary to explain why I think eating your food with more dedication and pleasure is so valuable. I grew up in the Netherlands, a country with a strong Calvinist tradition. Here, food has customarily been seen as a necessary evil and sex as an obligation to maintain the species. I feel a slight depression coming on as I write this. Let me explain anyway.

Of course, many people no longer see food and sex as a necessary evil. However, I can still sense this attitude in many people. They eat quickly, often behind the computer or in the car while driving. Research also suggests we are having less sex nowadays. I don't know whether the quality is less, but the moment you don't have it, I don't think you can enjoy it physically either. With such an attitude to life, enjoyment appears to be something reserved for special occasions. Sensual pleasure becomes a secret affair. Something from which you have to isolate yourself. A taboo. Salivating over a juicy peach that you eat slowly and lasciviously while its juice trickles down your chin is more likely to arouse disapproval than admiration.

Imagine making love to every apple or peanut butter sandwich. Truly, aware, loving, with red blushes, heavy breathing, and sensual thoughts. The submission connects all your senses: hearing, smell, touch, taste, your entire body. This feeling of your senses working in tandem allows you to reach and enjoy the deepest parts of your body. You just have to let it happen. We forget this is normal because we often fear others' disapproval. You are allowed to surrender to food's sensual pleasure.

You can use your natural tools (hands, lips and skin) when eating the following recipe. Kaye often serves it at her dinners. Here's how you eat it.

Place the yolk on your hand.

Enjoy the sensation of it sliding over your skin, then bite into it and lick the yolk off.

Alternatively, you can lick it off someone else's hand.

nude, slow-cooked egg yolks

- Preheat the oven to a low setting of approx. 55 °C. Fill a low oven dish with olive oil or rapeseed oil. Tip: The smaller the bowl, the less oil you need.
- Separate the eggs, leaving the yolk whole. Only use the egg yolks.
  Use the egg white for something else.
- Use a spoon to place the yolks into the oil carefully.
  Ensure the egg yolks are completely submerged in the oil; otherwise, they will dry out.
- Place the dish in the middle of the oven and confit the egg yolks for 60 minutes.
- The oil should not be too hot. You should be able to stick your finger in it easily.
  But it should not be too cold; otherwise, the yolks will not cook. If you have one,
  use a cooking thermometer to ensure the temperature is 55 °C.
- When the yolks are almost ready, massage a good olive oil or truffle oil (Kaye uses the latter) into the palms of your guests' hands.
- Carefully take the dish from the oven and remove the yolks one by one from the oil.
- Place a yolk on your guest's hands and sprinkle it with smoked salt.
- Invite your guests to eat the yolk off their own or each other's hands.
- The leftover oil can be filtered through a coffee filter and reused.
  You can infuse it with saffron, thyme or chilli and use the oil for your next dining experience.
  Make sure that the oil stays below 60 °C to maintain its quality.

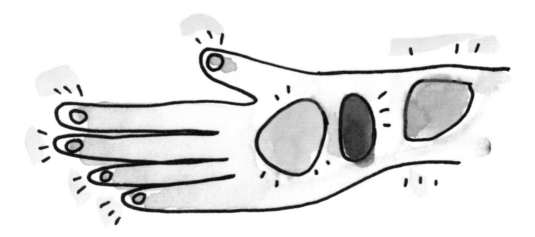

the eating human

I wonder, what is food anyway? Is it only digestible matter? Or is chewing gum also food? And what about clay? Pregnant women sometimes have a food craving called pica, where they eat clay. Is smoke also food? What do you think? What is food? Before you read on, write below the first answer that comes to mind.
I think food is:

Perhaps it is more interesting to ask yourself when something is food. And I'm talking about food for people. Otherwise, everything can be food. Some mushrooms, such as the Pestalotiopsis microspore, can even digest plastic. Not only does it eat plastic and live without oxygen, but it is also edible for humans. It offers us the chance to eat our plastic problem! Now, back to the question.

When is something food? Again, write below the first answer that comes to mind. Something is food when:

Isn't lettuce grown by a farmer food? Is wild lettuce also food? Maybe it is if you pluck it from the land. But when it grows in a ravine where no human ever goes, it is just a plant. It stands in all its solitary green glory, with only a woodlouse as a friend. (It's just like those miserable roadside weeds that no one notices.) Once it is food, that head of lettuce becomes 'foraged'. If you harvest, wash and prepare it with tomato and a tasty dressing, it's definitely food, right? But when the lettuce is left untouched on the table, it becomes waste. And if the lettuce is never harvested, it transforms into compost and becomes food for other organisms. A carrot skilfully cut into the shape of a flower or dragon can be eaten but usually remains as a garnish on the plate.

Lichen, those grey spots on trees, not to be confused with the cuddly moss, is edible. It's even very healthy. It grows everywhere, but I never see anyone gnawing it with their teeth off a tree's bark. A statue covered in lichen does not conjure up the idea of a tasty street buffet. The same applies to acorns, which do not end up on the dinner table but mainly on the autumn carpet.

My inner voice (the one that sounds like I just woke up with a hangover) says, 'What a load of nonsense. Who cares when something is food? As long as it tastes good, right?' That's true. Still, it is helpful for me to remember that food is only food when it is being eaten. At other times, it is 'solely' a plant, animal, fungus or algae. The world is full of edible plants and animals that we never consider taking a bite out of. And even if something is meant to be food, it can become something else – biofuel, for example.

Food's expressiveness is about more than just nutrition.

By picking something up, putting it into your mouth and swallowing it, you turn that thing into food. The moment something becomes food influences how I look at food. The eating human is not a machine. We are not like cars, which only need fuel to keep going. We are made of food. We live food. Food is us. We cannot separate ourselves from food. And when humans and food come together, they change each other. In the same way that a magic wand is merely a stick when no wizard or witch is around, edible organisms are just plants or animals until someone decides to take a bite out of them. Only then does the plant transform into a magical object and thus into real food. The ring, which could lie in the river for years, only began to exert its dark influence when Smeagol found it. Harry's invisibility cloak is not invisible until it is used. When not in use, the cloak is a mere piece of fabric. (Where does Harry keep that thing anyway?)

But when Harry wears it, the cloak changes, and he does too. Harry not only becomes invisible but also does things his visible self wouldn't do. He makes different choices and sees other possibilities. His thoughts change because he knows he's wearing the cloak. Although the cloak is a functional object that Harry uses, the cloak also affects him. Similarly, we influence how the world looks through what we eat, but food also influences us. And I'm not just talking about beer bellies and six-packs. Food's expressiveness is about more than feeding your body. Which, in itself, if you stop to think about it, is already a magical experience.

Food isn't food until you put it in your mouth.
Your mouth, that soft, warm, agile opening filled with enamelled weapons, is the gateway to a whole human being – a person with feelings and ideas. Food is the organism you bite into, and it is what connects humans and organisms. This is what I consider to be food. You can give two people the same cookie, but they will taste and experience it differently. As well as the two people's characters, the time of day and location can also influence their divergent cookie experiences. A cookie tastes different at a funeral in the rain than lying on a sunny lawn. A product may be measurably and objectively the same, but the people who eat it are always different. We cannot perceive food objectively without expectations, associations, fantasies and emotions. What's the point of looking at food as an isolated phenomenon if we can't perceive it objectively? What is food without the eating human?

Imagine you are fired on a rough day, and you catch your loved one with someone else, and then, to make matters worse, you step in dog poo just before dinner at a Michelin-starred restaurant. The food can objectively still be delicious. Nevertheless, the chances are you won't get maximum enjoyment out of the food. If on another day, however, you fall head over heels in love and win the lottery and then hop through the park hungry, and all you can find is a stall selling revolting, flaccid hot dogs, it will probably taste delicious. You might even eat it more often because it reminds you of that beautiful moment in your life. Is a hot dog better than a refined Michelin-star dish? Yes, for this person, it is. If food is not 'just' food but represents the relationship between humans and the eaten organism, it represents something of a challenge. It makes food a complex subject because how can a cook take all these things into account when cooking for someone? You don't know what the diner thinks and feels and has experienced that day, do you? Do you really have to take this into account? Ultimately, you have better and more important things to do! Besides, people often do not know what emotions they are experiencing and where they come from.

Food may be the key to unlocking hidden memories.

A project I did demonstrated how emotions, food and memories are inextricably linked. I prepared dishes from the Dutch Second World War famine of 1944–1945 (known as the Hongerwinter) and served them to people who grew up at that time. I made 'Valsch Vleesch' (Fake Meat) from mashed white beans and a type of red beet rösti called 'Hendrik de Hongerdoder' (Hendrich the Hunger Killer). I also served tulip bulbs and sugar beet as if they were stewed pears. Some of the participants hadn't tasted these dishes for over sixty-five years. They took a bite, and lo and behold, the magical object came to life. It transported the diners back to the war, to their kitchens with their brothers and sisters, their parents still alive. They remembered sounds, smells, moments and experiences they had forgotten. The 1940 bombardment of Rotterdam caused black ash to fall in the city for days. The kids called it 'black confetti'. These memories had been locked away in their heads for years; the food had been the key to unlocking them. Although some of the memories were painful, they also aroused a meaningful experience. The vivid memory, evoked by the Proust effect (see chapter Smell), transformed sugar beet normally used for animal feed into a magical and meaningful dish.

These memories did not occur for all of the diners, because they grew up in a different cultural background, or their mothers might have used a different recipe. 'Have a handful of cumin seeds,' Tony's mother used to say when the children complained of hunger. 'And go to sleep quickly, then you won't feel so bad.' A handful of cumin seeds was not on my menu. So it is pretty challenging working with food because you never know what the diner thinks and feels. The particular experience of the eating human is immeasurable. This indeterminable quality is problematic when cooking for someone, but it also offers many possibilities. If you stop looking at food as an objective product and start thinking about it as a magical object – the key to transformation – you go from being a Muggle to a wizard.

So, if food is about the relationship between you and what you eat, let's look at you, **the eating human.**

Fill in the details below.
name: date:

Yersterday I ate:

Describe the situation in which you ate and with whom:

As a child, I often ate:

Describe the situation and surroundings you were in:

Describe the taste sensation and texture of your favourite food:

Describe the taste sensation and texture of your least favourite food:

If you had to think of a word for the feeling you get in your mouth when you eat your favourite food, what would it be? And for your least favourite food?

Can you remember the smell of the kitchen from your childhood? Try to describe it. If you can't, then try to remember the smell of someone else's kitchen:

What did you eat secretly as a child when your parents weren't looking? Describe how that felt and tasted:

What did you take to eat on a school trip?

Do you know what it feels like to cry and eat at the same time?
What had happened, and what did it taste like?

What food did you love as a child but don't eat anymore?
What did you like about it, and why don't you eat it anymore?

Do you remember losing your milk teeth? Can you describe the feeling of eating without a
tooth or teeth? Did you play with food between your teeth?

Did you learn to drink coffee, tea or alcohol? Do you remember when it happened? Describe the situation:

Are there any flavours or dishes that you couldn't imagine ever eating as a child but that you eat now? Describe how you imagined the taste, smell, and texture as a child.

Have you ever argued about food? Why and with whom did you argue? What food was it?

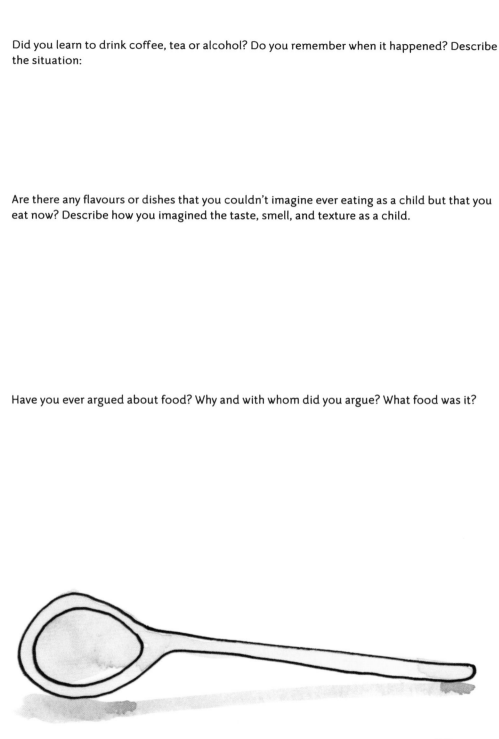

What do you eat when you are sick? Who shared this knowledge with you?

Is there a food you adore because someone you like enjoys it?
Who is it, and what food is it?

Do you ever lie about what you eat? What is the lie?

Have you ever felt embarrassed because you ate certain foods at an important moment?
Describe the situation.

What do you like most about eating?

What do you dislike about eating?

If you could invent a new kind of edible plant, what would it look like, and how would it grow?
What would it taste like, and what would you make with it? What is the plant called?

this is no Brussel's Sprout.
this is a chocolate ball.

What do you want to be when you grow down?

shrink

He served a whole ostrich and white cabbage. Whole, white cabbages. His guests sat around the table and had shrunk to a height of fifty centimetres. Now, they were gnomes looking at a large steaming bowl of roast chicken and Brussels sprouts.

Arne had told them about his idea. People have grown increasingly tall in recent decades. What if, instead of growing, we shrunk? And preferably to fifty centimetres high, about the size of a newborn baby.

No, not you. Not in your lifetime.

However, if our offspring were to get a little shorter gradually, we could grow steadily smaller, instead of increasingly larger, until we become a miniature species. Consider, for example, how some dog breeds have been bred to be smaller. It may seem an unalterable law to us that all living things only grow and never shrink, but there are animals that, depending on the circumstances, can either shrink or grow. For example, an adult marine iguana from the Galapagos Islands can shrink by up to twenty per cent when food is scarce. Salmon, too, can shrink in the winter, only to grow again in warmer months.

For us humans, growth is such a given that we generally don't take the idea of shrinkage seriously. We are obsessed with growth because bigger often seems better. People are getting taller, but that's not all. We are growing larger vegetables and eating larger portions. Did you know that along with our hunger for growth, our tableware has increased in size over the last sixty years? Take a look in an antique shop, and you'll see we now classify an antique dinner plate as a breakfast plate. Even the Eames dining room chair, which has become a design classic, is slightly bigger than the original. We are growing in width as well as in height.

The only thing that doesn't grow proportional to height is longevity.

A possible explanation for our growth may lie in better nutrition and our desire for big, bigger, biggest. We consider height to be attractive. We take taller people more seriously than their shorter counterparts. Tall people – especially men – enjoy more prestige. Out of necessity, they also enjoy more food because their larger bodies need more fuel to function properly. The only thing that doesn't grow proportional to height is longevity. For every centimetre people are taller than 1.52 metres, they live six months less. In all respects, the taller your body, the less durable you are.

Our nutritional needs grow or shrink exponentially to our height. Thus, for every twenty per cent we are shorter, we only need half as much food. A fifty-centimetre-tall person would need approximately sixty calories daily – the equivalent of one apple a day. And it is only two per cent of a six-foot-tall adult's calorie needs, who would need forty-six apples a day to live. Our current average portion would feed about fifty small people. Now imagine that you and everyone else on your street were only fifty centimetres tall. Then you all – two hundred people – eat one chicken. A roast chicken on the table would look as large and plentiful as an ostrich. One tiny sprout would then be the size of a whole cabbage!

Did you ever see at close quarters how enormous an ostrich is? Years ago, I prepared a dinner in South Africa where I wrapped ostriches in clay, cooked them in a 'ground oven', and then served them. Two birds fed a hundred people, and still much was left over. The local ostrich farmer said the ostriches in South Africa were not kept for their meat but mainly for their feathers, of which a big buyer is Brazil, where they feature in the ornaments for the annual carnival. Ostrich leather is used for bags. Their meat was a by-product of the feather and leather industry and was initially hardly eaten. It was only when ostrich steaks started appearing on the menus of luxury restaurants in Europe that the meat also increased in price.

Then there are the ostriches' eggs. The birds lay about fifty eggs a year, and each egg weighs one and a half kilos, which is equivalent to about twenty-five chicken eggs. This means you can cook a stack of seventy pancakes with one ostrich egg. What an abundance from just one egg!

But rather than keeping more ostriches to obtain greater abundance, we need to consider the opposite approach because more ostriches require more ostrich food and more land. If we shrunk, we could make a correspondingly large stack of pancakes from one chicken egg.

The moment you downsize, the world instantly offers more abundance.

Now imagine how much more space you would have if you were smaller. You would need less water, less food, less raw materials, less house and, therefore, less heat. The moment you downsize, the world instantly offers more abundance. We cannot make Earth bigger, but our planet proportionately grows when we shrink.

'So that's the great paradox!' Arne exclaims.
By taking a step back and not constantly striving for more, you will ultimately achieve more. Our mental growth is significant in grasping this task. Arne Hendriks is an artistic researcher who lives in Amsterdam and has been working on 'The Incredible Shrinking Man' concept since 2010. For Arne, shrinking is both fantasy and utopia. 'I'm 1.95 metres tall and very aware of this. I often feel clumsy because I take up so much space.' His work draws on his fondness for storytelling, and he applies his artistic imagination to develop his shrinking humanity concept. Thus he combines scientific research, fantasy and curiosity into a new narrative. 'We still believe, albeit without any critical thinking, that growing bigger is the right thing to do, but we have to ask ourselves whether this is really the case.'

Arne often uses food as a means to tell his stories. He calculated, for example, that a cup of coffee for a fifty-centimetre-tall person can be made from precisely one coffee bean. And growing one bean needs about three and a half litres of water. Compare that to the forty coffee beans and 140 litres of water we now need for each cup. Our worldwide coffee consumption consumes 110 trillion cubic metres of fresh water every year: as much as flows through the Rhine in a year and a half. A 'food lens' helps you to understand the actual implications of shrinkage better, Arne thinks. Nevertheless, one coffee bean for one cup of coffee per person does have a poetic quality. We can always relate to food.

It's not impossible. We can become smaller.
Just as we have grown, Arne says. We can reverse this trend. The question is whether it is possible and why we don't try. Is it because we are obsessed with growth? Just as we desire and expect growth from our economic system and how much we produce. But is this realistic if our space does not grow likewise? Can we change our desire? Can we also long for reduction and down-sizing? 'The literal idea of shrinking may sound like a childlike fantasy', says Arne. 'But if you take this fantasy seriously, you will discover a whole world behind it.'

As much as we are obsessed with growth, many are also passionate about miniaturisation – model trains, for instance, or YouTube channels dedicated to preparing tiny meals. Japan has a cultural preference and sensitivity for small things, such as bonsai trees and small carved netsuke ornaments. Even sushi is a kind of miniature food. Miniaturisation is funny, crazy and entertaining, but we don't take it seriously. Whereas growth is prestigious and shows potential, shrinkage is inferior and infantile. Shrinking provides for amusing stories in books and films, such as Gulliver's Travels, Alice in Wonderland and Honey, I Shrunk the Kids. Nevertheless, NASA is investigating the possibilities of and for shrinking. Indeed, every extraneous gram on a trip to Mars costs a fortune in fuel, food, water and oxygen.

Shrinkage is inferior. Nevertheless, NASA is investigating the possibilities of shrinking.

Although Arne was initially mainly concerned with small things, he gradually realised that growth and shrinkage implicitly affect almost every aspect of our lives. 'When I discovered that small potato fries in tiny bags cook much faster – only needing fifteen seconds per chip – I became acquainted with economic growth and contraction. I investigated this issue further when I was an artist in residence for Rabobank and discovered that ships full of grain sail the oceans but never reach the coast. They are speculative objects. Most people think of food as providing for our basic needs, but it is also the biggest economic driver and a vehicle for economic growth. Some wines are bottled and bought for 100,000 euros a bottle, but they are never drunk.'

Cancer grows, but we would rather see it shrink.
Arne compares our obsession with growth to cancer: it grows and takes over until it consumes you. He worked with geneticist, physician and professor of Molecular Genetics, Hans Clevers. Together they looked at cancer's rampant growth in the body. Hans said he comes up with all kinds of theories and ideas during his research, but ultimately, he always comes back to the human cell. There lies the answer, and it is there that he sees whether his theory is correct. This idea – the cell as a yardstick – keeps him modest. Arne wonders whether this idea would also work for economists. What is their 'living cell' against which they test their theories, that keeps them humble, and that shows whether their thoughts align with the measure of humans and nature?

When it is us who shrink, we can experience more abundance. But can this also be translated to the economy? What if the principle of less growth could also lead to a greater sense of wealth? And what if we replace 'more' with 'less'? Perhaps this would allow us more space for other things, such as time, rest, and satisfaction

hara hachi bu
On the Japanese island of Okinawa, people don't say 'itadaki mas' (thanks for the food). They are more likely to say 'hara hachi bu'. Besides being a salutation, hara hachi bu serves as advice and a way of life. It means 'eat until you are eighty per cent full'. Thus, you have twenty per cent space left over: twenty per cent 'residual space'.

Ideally, this philosophy is not only applied to food but to all aspects of life. Fill your calendar eighty per cent and keep twenty per cent free. Creating or reserving space is at least as important as filling it. If you fill your week, it is to the detriment of your flexibility and freedom. If you overindulge, you are more likely to develop an aversion to the foods you eat too much of. You feel bloated and can't move another step. Our bodies seem to work much better when we keep twenty per cent of our stomach empty.

Take a step back and see: there is more space left in front of you.

Arne cites the hara hachi bu principle to demonstrate what can happen if you stop striving for maximum growth. Instead of moving forward, take a step back and observe: more space remains in front of you. Hara hachi bu is an exercise in creating space. Space for yourself. Space for something else. Space for someone else. This is why Arne used to carry small cutlery always. 'When I ate with a small fork and spoon, it completely changed my experience. A tomato seed became a fisheye in green jelly on my mini-spoon. Seashells such as cockles are often pricked with a pin and eaten, providing a different eating experience. Your sensitivity changes.' Similarly, your experience of eating an amuse-bouche is different to eating a bowl of stew. Though they may use the same ingredients, a small 'sample' has a different value than an 'all you can eat'. You become your own magnifying glass through such experiences. By zooming in, you discover a different world that reveals a beauty and richness separate from the world you experience from a zoomed-out, more distant position. Such a change in attitude is specifically what Arne's work pursues. 'I want to change people's perspectives so that they subsequently experience more space.'

from the moment he started eating potato crisps with a pin he lost weight.

You can read more about Arne Hendriks' research into the shrinking human being and its implications at the-incredible-shrinking-man.net

challenge

put a stone in your soup

Around the world, most people eat about ten per cent more than necessary. This is shocking when you consider that many people still consistently lack food. You can regard overeating as a form of food waste. Moreover, it has negative consequences for your health.

In a world of abundance, 'less' is a dirty word.
It turns out that our eyes can't properly judge how much food is on our plates. An infamous study by the University of Wageningen demonstrated that we keep eating soup that is surreptitiously refilled via a tube at the bottom of the bowl. We will happily eat double the amount under such circumstances before we decide to stop. And if you are a fast eater, you will often eat beyond the point of being full because it takes twenty minutes for your stomach to realise it has had enough.

Finish your plate!
Who didn't hear this as a child? Many adults are therefore used to eating everything on their plate without grumbling, even when it's too much food. So, how do you prevent this? You can eat from a smaller plate, which makes it look fuller. You can eat your soup from smaller bowls with a smaller spoon. Hence you take smaller mouthfuls and eat slower, which allows you the necessary time to feel when you are full.

You can also put inedible things on your plate that resemble food. I once made porcelain and stone objects with a silicone shell that had the abstract appearance of food. They had organic protrusions and looked edible – or lickable. I discovered that if you put such things among the food on your plate, your mind thinks the plate is full – which it is, but not with food.

Another consequence of placing objects on your plate is you start playing with them. Try putting some olives on that beautiful stone you found on vacation, or put some pieces of cucumber against it. You become aware of the elements on your plate and start styling it, as it were. You might say – as my mother used to – 'it doesn't matter what it looks like, because it all ends up in one mass in your stomach', but this is simply not true. Besides this being a disheartening view, food actually starts with the eyes. Your eyes 'eat' your food before it even enters your mouth. The Japanese call this 'the shape of taste'. You eat with more attention from a beautifully presented dish. Paying more attention causes you to eat slower, and you are less likely to overeat.

try it yourself

You don't need specially designed ceramic objects to fill your plate. A rock, shell, or upside-down cup or egg cup on your plate has the same effect. Make sure everything is clean and then work as a stylist would. Put your food on your plate between your objects, using a little less than you would normally. You'll notice it's pretty crazy and sometimes even irritating having a stone in your soup or eating a pasta dish that you can't just spoon in mindlessly. Above all, check out the reactions from your fellow tablemates. You'll notice the dining experience is very different.

Don't forget to share your photos on instagram: **@lickit.book**

Hurry!

time

I thought Mark just didn't like pears, but, it turns out, he has a deep-seated hatred for them. 'You can't trust them!' he says as if talking about emails in which you've inherited another million. I look surprised. I often eat pears because I'm allergic to apples. I especially like the harder pears that still resemble an apple. Mark looks at it with utter contempt.

British comedian Eddie Izzard voices his feelings about the pear. 'They are beautiful little things, those pears, but they are only ripe for half an hour. They're either like a rock, or they're mush. In the supermarket, people hammer nails into them; they're that hard! I take them home so they can ripen in peace. And they sit there going, "No. No. Don't ripen yet. Don't ripen yet. Wait until he goes out of the room...." And then I leave, and they yell, "NOW, guys! Ripen, now, now, now!" And you come back in and think, "Oh good, I'll just have a pear." You reach into the fruit bowl and get a hand full of mush. This unpredictable transience of pears also provokes intense frustration in Mark. In a quasi-hypocritical manner, Mark likes pear ice cream because then the 'soft mush' texture makes sense.

Modern life has few phenomena that so powerfully remind us of time as food's impermanence. Although we slowly decay every day, it happens gradually. We don't sit in the fridge to preserve ourselves for longer. We know life is temporary. Even so, we do our best to stay young as long as possible. We prefer to be eternally youthful in denial of life's natural passage. We surround ourselves with static objects. Outside, clouds drift by, and summer slowly makes way for autumn; but inside, time seems to stand still. The table remains a table. The spoons remain spoons. Perhaps the computer lags behind the rapidly developing pace of technology, but it remains a computer. Unmoved by the cycle of life, the objects around us reflect a timeless vacuum. We look from the inside out of our timeless capsule and observe, 'Oh, it's night again,' and turn out the lights.

We prefer to think of food as being like the other things around us: static and everlasting.

Nevertheless, time is present in our 'inner world'. Indeed, time has us firmly in its grip – but it is a different time. It is an imaginary time formed by agreements we made or were made for us. Time to go to work, time to catch the train, time for a new phone because my subscription is about to expire. Time, made visible by the clock and calendar, is broken down into bite-sized chunks of months, weeks, hours and minutes. Kronos, a Greek titan and father of Zeus, represents clock time, order, structure and the chronological passage of time. He ate his children for fear of the future, just as time itself eats life. People often fear time slipping away and live trapped in clock time, making them feel disconnected from life. This kind of time, born of Earth's revolutions but cultivated into a rigid tyrant, has a more significant influence on our daily lives than the cycles of birth, life and death. There is little you can do about either type of time. And though you cannot plan the spring season to the minute, it comes, like death, of its own accord. Likewise, six o'clock will come round again, without anyone's help. As well as these types of time, there is your own sense of time. My son started the countdown to his tenth birthday three months before. Those three months were arguably the longest and worst of his entire life. As the revered date of his birthday drew nearer, the days crept by even more slowly. He grew tired of the wait and almost lost all interest. 'Forget about the stupid birthday!' he said resentfully. He forgot about the count-down, and the day shot toward him and flew by like a rubber band. 'The day only lasted an hour,' he said, looking back.

Kairos represents our inner sense of time.
Kairos is the youngest son of Zeus and grandson of Kronos. On his bald head grows one lock of hair that you can grab when the right moment comes: thus, you seize the moment. Kairos represents your inner sense of time, inspiration and the opportune flow of time and place. It is the opposite of Kronos, the chronological passage of time. Kairos is about the crucial moment

rather than continuous time and connects you to the feeling of being alive. But what does this have to do with food? Even though we seem to be in a kind of still life with all those inanimate objects around us, food connects us with nature's cycles and out inner sense of time several times a day. We eat something that is somewhere between birth and a state of decomposition. We eat a seed that can still grow into a whole plant. We eat fruit that grew from a flower and slowly ripened in the sun. Somewhere in the process of germination and wilting, you intervene and stop time. Each stage of growth brings with it different flavours. Do you eat a pumpkin seed, a flower from the pumpkin or the fruit itself? You can store seeds for a long time, but flowers can wilt within a day. Decay also sets in with the harvest – and we don't want that. We prefer to see food like everything else we surround ourselves with: static and everlasting.

Drying, smoking and pickling all serve to delay the effects of time.

You might say, 'Oh, there's another story about how we modern people want to bend life to our will.' But this isn't necessarily a present-day thing. Since time immemorial, prolonging food's shelf life has been a vital activity. Drying, smoking, pickling, canning, sugaring, oiling, cooling and fermenting were invented all over the world in the distant past to delay the effects of time and decay. Since the industrial revolution, other techniques have been introduced and applied on a large scale. First, there was pasteurisation and canning, then more advanced techniques such as vacuum packing, replacing air with gas in the packaging, chemical preservatives, irradiation and freeze-drying. And there are many more ways we curb food from spoiling. Looking around the supermarket, you will see things frozen in time. (See chapter Small Blocks.) Nearly all the products stand there like petrified monuments made from raw materials that once grew in a field or on a plantation. They sprouted, the rain drizzled down on them, and the sun warmed them up. Insects crawled by or landed on their leaves as their roots made their way through the dark soil. The supermarket products are just like the time of Kronos. They are originally natural but 'trapped' in a system of hours and minutes so that order and control now dominate.

During the COVID-19 lockdown, Ramona Morales took my Advanced Food and Design Dive course online from her apartment in Chile. She showed me images of a bathtub full of tomatoes and a bed full of apples. Ramona had collected and preserved rejected fruits and vegetables from the local market. 'What a job that was,' she sighed. But it was worth it because she saved nearly sixty kilos of fruit and vegetables from the compost heap. She had stopped time just before the decay kicked in, which also took much of her time. She calculated how much time it took to make a jar of tomato sauce, factoring in her time spent and the growing time. But what is the starting point? Do you start with the seed? She made labels for her jars showing the time it had taken to produce the product. Grilled Eggplant took 4320 growing hours to grow, three hours to save them, two hours and fifty-one minutes to prepare them, and fifty-five minutes to preserve them. Finally, she factored in another thirty-five minutes for eating them. That's a lot of time packed into a small jar of grilled aubergines. What would you do if you received this time in your life as a gift?

Time is measurable but invisible.

Time is an ingredient. A typical recipe might need fifty grams of cheese, one hundred grams of flour, butter, a pinch of salt and thirty minutes. The element of time considerably influences the taste of food. You have young and old cheese, matured whiskey or fresh sashimi. Yet 'time' is never written on your shopping list underneath the toilet paper and carrots. You may be thinking, 'That's because time is free and you can't buy it in a shop.' If time is something everyone simply has, why do so many people think they never have enough of it? We often don't have enough time to cook or enjoy a nice meal. If you have time to immerse yourself in videos of screaming huskies on TikTok for half an hour every day, you probably also have time to cook. So it's not time that you lack but rather motivation and energy. It may feel like you don't have the time because there is more to do in your life. Because you have options. If you have little cooking experience, it can feel like a big job beforehand, while – timed to the minute – it's not that bad. For a while, I was so preoccupied with work and children that I felt like I didn't even have time to clean the toilet. I started thinking of it as a monumental task. So I timed how long it took me to clean: five minutes. After that, I could always find the time to do it. Sometimes you have to be rational about time. If you don't have a clock, you can do what people did before they were invented and use other markers of time. Some old cookbooks indicate cooking times with a number of Hail Marys.

Time may be free, but it is also priceless.
Time is free, yet time is money. You can buy time if you have enough money – the time to grow food, gather together or cook. You only have to do the 'heavy work' of eating yourself. It's nice not to cook for yourself now and then. However, you miss out on the 'IKEA effect' whereby you like something more if you've made it yourself. (See chapter Gratis.) If you put in the effort to cook your food – or even grow it – you will enjoy the result more. Mark's father doesn't grow pears, but he grows all his own vegetables, saving him a lot of money. Although this also takes time, it doesn't feel that way because it's his hobby. The difference is rather than 'costing' time, you 'invest' time and get pleasure in return and, in this case, vegetables too. He grows kilos of tomatoes, and none of them goes to waste. He recently gave Mark a tomato plant for me, but unfortunately, the plant arrived damaged. It was as if one of his children had pulled an arm out of its socket. At least that's how it felt to his father, who had put time and attention into raising the plant. Time and attention also transform what might otherwise be meaningless things in the world around you into small wonders. The tomato plant remains a tomato plant, but a home-grown plant is instinctively different.

Designers Lucas Mullié and Digna Kosse work as a duo called Foodcurators. In 2011, they opened a restaurant called Tijdrestaurant (Time Restaurant) that proved that though time is invisible, it is very tangible. They lined the restaurant's walls with large shelving units filled with a 'collection' made up of 'culinary capsules'. The capsules were large jars that put time on hold for all kinds of food. Lucas and Digna also made edible fossils from dried products, such as salt plates with fish and enfleurage with flowers in fat. Their fascination with the pausing of food and shutting off external influences so that time stands still meant they could phase out the refrigerator after a few weeks. Refrigerators continuously consume energy and are therefore not a truly effective form of preservation. They compiled a menu based on the collection, and you could combine ingredients from different seasons. They sent part of the collection to the Victoria & Albert Museum in London for a capsule lunch. It might not sound extraordinary to combine ingredients from different seasons, because we take for granted the all-year-round availability of products. Do you know when 'cauliflower season' is? Or apple season? If you stop and think about it, a dessert with strawberries and plums is exceptional in Western Europe. Without a greenhouse or refrigerator, strawberries and plums only have a few weeks of concurrent ripeness.

When I had my first restaurant in Rotterdam, some customers were irritated that we had run out of delicious slow-food goat cheeses. Riled, they declared they had come all the way from Groningen just for the cheese. I explained to the displeased people that the cheeses were gone because we needed to wait for the milk to become available again. And for that, the goats had to get pregnant again and give birth. Providing this explanation was the best thing to do. Especially if customers have made a goat's cheese pilgrimage from Groningen. In such moments, you realise food is part of the unshakeable essence of cyclical time and plays with people's personal sense of time.

Do something you enjoy, grab Kairos by his lock of hair and slow down time.

Whether you are eating something that will soon spoil or something so preserved that it stops you from getting wrinkles, your individual perception of time is always present when you eat. Time, in one way or another, affects your eating. If you start to see time as an invisible but tangible ingredient, you can use it intentionally. Think of it as comparable to sound. Sound is always present around you. Sometimes, it bothers you; sometimes, you enjoy it. The same is true of time. Time can get the better of you, but you can also use it to your advantage, such as by cooking and eating with undivided attention. You only have twenty-four hours in a day, but if you're doing something you enjoy and with complete dedication, you can grab Kairos by his lock of hair, extend time like warm toffee, and balance on the slowly stretching thread. Doing so allows you to turn an hour into a whole season.

challenge

edible time capsule

I read a news article that supermarket minced meat is sometimes ten years old. It has been frozen all that time and is still perfectly edible. This thought excites me. Our preservation techniques allow us to time travel! The animals living then had never heard of COVID-19.

So how about your freezer? Does it also contain things from the previous decade?
Let's make a time capsule with our freezer.

how?

- Go outside and see if you can pick or gather anything edible (nettles, chestnuts, edible flowers or, if it's the deep midwinter, snow!) If you are unsure what is edible, look for foraging apps and websites for your region.
- Clean your harvest, if necessary, put it in a freezer bag, and write the date on it.
- Tear the following page from this book and fill in the questionnaire on the front and back with a ballpoint pen or permanent marker.
- Search online for a simple recipe using the things you've harvested and write it on the back of the torn-out page.
- Put the page in the bag, and put it in the back of your freezer.
- If you use a calendar app, put an appointment in it for the same day in three years, at which point you shall make the recipe from the bag and – while eating your dish – read the accompanying note.
- If you move house before the three-year period has elapsed, you can cook your time capsule earlier and eat it among the moving boxes.

what is this bag doing in my freezer?

You have probably discovered this note three years after putting it in your freezer. It was one of the challenges from that strange book by Marije Vogelzang, remember? On this day, three years ago, you foraged food and put it in your freezer. On the back of this note is the recipe you will be making. Before you read on below, make the recipe with the ingredients from this bag. Then read the letter below while eating the food you froze three years ago. Do you remember what the world was like then?

Dear   (your name)

I am happy that you have found this time capsule. Today it is   in the year

In my life right now, I am mostly occupied with

and

I am worried about

I'm looking forward to

What I'd like to remind you of is

In three years, I hope my life will be

I wish for you

Here is the recipe you can make with these found ingredients.
Good luck, and enjoy your meal!

what if?

I was once visiting a couple who had one of those large apple juice cartons. You know the ones – the cardboard kind with a plastic bag and a tap. You open the tap, the pack slowly empties, and there's a vacuum inside so that the juice has a longer shelf life. Unfortunately, the tap leaked.

The pack contained several litres of apple juice, and they didn't drink that much, so these people had devised a device for catching the drips. They had hung a metal wire from the tap with a dish underneath it. With each new drop that fell, the dish amassed an increasing puddle of juice. It was summer, and a colony of fruit flies had contentedly established itself on the dish. Although they (the couple, not the fruit flies) cleaned it regularly, there was also a fruit fly trap next to the pack to be safe. Problem solved!

Then their son came in. He saw the dripping tap, smiled at his parents and removed the bowl. He grabbed the pack with both hands and set it on its back. Now the tap wasn't under the pressure of the juice, so it didn't leak.

In my design work, I want to come up with ideas that lead you off the beaten track. In the creative process, I look for alternative perspectives. We consider so many things normal in this world when they may not be at all.

If you live somewhere where drinking water comes from the tap, I wonder how many times you have got down on your knees in front of the tap to express your gratitude. You probably think tap water is quite normal, even though it is something of a miracle that it flows into your home affordable and clean. Though we consider this provision very normal, most people also think of water as something to be economically and sustainably conserved. Yet most of us flush clean drinking water down the toilet, bathe in it, and wash the car with it. We are like a modern Louis XIV. We live in luxury without realising it – as if we were eating and pooping out gold. Incidentally, I just read that the Sun King liked to eat salad with tarragon and basil all year round and preferably garnished atop with violets.

By presenting something as ordinary as tap water as wine, you change the context.

I once came up with a National Tap Water Tasting Event, where I collected tap water from every province in the Netherlands and had it set out for people to taste as if it were a wine tasting event. Wine is often treated as a kind of sacred liquid. People will spend excessive amounts of money on wine. Wine has special glasses for every type, and there are rituals associated with its tasting with beautiful and charming descriptions of the taste and smell. For example, the term 'terroir' refers to the fact that you can taste, among other things, the soil in which the vine was grown.

When we talk about water, it is mainly about saving or not saving it and whether we are paying too much for it. I don't hear many people discussing the taste of water. And if they do, it is with a limited vocabulary that extends no further than 'tasty' or perhaps 'dirty'. (We seem to express our displeasure more often than our pleasure.) Even so, water also has a 'terroir', and different types of water have different pH values and mineral ratios. By presenting something as ordinary as tap water as wine, you change the context. In doing so, you create the opportunity to appreciate its taste and realise how special it is that we have tap water. Daring to think differently can 'ignite' a spark of realisation. To achieve this, you must first approach something with a questioning attitude and interrogate it.

pray for me

Questions in and of themselves do not always lead to answers.
Or perhaps they do, but does the answer provide the impetus for the next step? Isn't the solution just the start of a new problem? Fertiliser was the answer to a question and a solution to a problem, but then it became the problem. Sometimes there is even a solution first and then the problem. As Joseph Weizenbaum points out, body odour only became a problem after the invention of deodorant.

What if...
food was so modified that it could crawl off your plate like a living creature?
What if...
we made lichen a daily part of our diet?
What if...
all food was free?
What if...
you were only allowed to eat meat from animals you raise and slaughter yourself?
What if...
sweets were healthy and even medicinal?
What if...
you had to grow all your food on a square metre of land next to your house?
What if...
you only had salt water for crop cultivation?
What if...
you got all your nutrients from a drink while having a supercool eating experience through a hyper-realistic computer simulation?

What would you do?
What would that be like?
And why are you reading a book that asks you all these questions?

When looking for a solution to a problem, you are likely to think, 'How? How do I solve this?' A how question activates your brain's logical thinking ability because your brain produces beta brain waves. Your brain becomes alert and thinks, 'Hey, a puzzle. Let me find the solution as efficiently as possible.' Questions with how help solve practical problems.

If you want to know the fastest way to get through IKEA because you have to be back in time to pick up your kids from school, it's helpful if your brain uses beta waves. These waves help you focus and solve specific problems, so you don't lie on a SÄBÖVIK bed and daydream about all the possibilities for walking through IKEA. Possibilities such as:
- Give everything with an Ö a kiss and take the route with the most kisses;
- Sing, walking backwards from the entrance, shove a Swedish meatball in the mouth of other people's children until you are escorted out of the building;

- Give other shoppers a paper tape measure, close your eyes and ask them to blindly guide you like a dog on a leash until you reach the exit. Once there, start whining and ask them to buy you an ice cream.

If you have children who like to be picked up from school on time, then questions with how are handy because your brain goes into 'solve mode'. This also works for why questions. Such questions require explanations, like a three-year-old who keeps asking 'why'. You have no choice but to explain. No matter how philosophical the questions are – such as 'Why is lettuce alive?' – you are bound to attempt an answer, even if it's 'Because that's the way it is!' Formulating an answer is almost imperative. After that, you are done and can move on to the next thing. That's why specific answers seldom lead to new ideas because our heads treat the matter as closed and solved.

tapwine

baby tears

If we are looking for a different take on food, we have to think differently. And to start thinking differently, we have to ask different questions.

Angling for immediate answers and solutions is useful for life's everyday practicalities. Because you then know why, for example, people become overweight (because they overeat ultra-processed food) and how you can change that (they have to eat less). But has anything really changed? Everyone knows that overeating makes you overweight and that it is healthier to eat less processed foods. But apparently, knowing the solution doesn't stop people from becoming overweight. Knowing the solution is not the same as solving the problem. By continuing to think logically, you constantly come up with the same answers and solutions.

What if we did not need to think logically to free ourselves from existing thought patterns? If everything could be solved logically, why hasn't it all been solved by all those logical thinking people working with food? I'm not saying logical thinking isn't valuable, but only at the right time. To return to my own working method, it is only after I have determined my vision – by treating water as wine, for example (Jesus didn't always think logically either)– do I engage my logical thinking ability. Then I will think about how to make an installation in which I fill 360 one-litre bottles per Dutch province with water. Why 360 litres? Because the average Dutch person uses 360 litres of water per day: very logical.

Only after determining my vision do I engage my logical thinking ability.

For a different perspective on food, you first need a different vision. Only then do you have the logical brainpower to answer the how questions and shape your vision. Perhaps you don't need expensive technical solutions or significant investments for this at all. Maybe it's much more straightforward than that.

To think differently, you should ask different questions so your head doesn't immediately go into 'solve mode'. When your head is in solve mode, you have a one-sided view of your problem: you only look straight at it. It's comparable to standing in front of a mountain and looking at the summit. You think about how to get there but only see the path in front of the mountain. You only see what seems most logical. It might not occur to you that there could be a cable car at the back of the mountain or a free helicopter service with champagne and a massage. You also do not see what the mountain top looks like. Hungry, man-eating kittens may be waiting for you. And that phenomenal view you so longed for, you might find it underneath instead of on top of the mountain, in a cavity full of sparkling gemstones. Perhaps the path in front of you is the right path to take but not fit to walk. You may even destroy the mountain by climbing it.

Sometimes what you see in front of you doesn't make the most sense. Sometimes it's better to look at something from multiple angles. Then you will see you don't have to attach contraptions to an apple juice carton's leaking tap, but you can stop the leak by placing the pack on its side.

Activating your alpha brainwaves lets your thoughts skip around without a leash.

Ask yourself different questions and give yourself the opportunity to move beyond what seems initially logical. Questions starting with 'What if...?' or 'What would it be like if...?' allow you the freedom to explore. They pause your 'logical brain' so you don't have to devise a solution immediately. You want to summon the alpha brainwaves rather than the beta ones. If you train yourself to fantasise without distraction or start a sentence with 'what if', you will often find yourself in this alpha-wave state. It's similar to daydreaming: you're awake, but you let your thoughts skip around without a leash. You allow your mind to make connections that are improbable or don't immediately make sense. However, these thoughts can be very valuable. If you've ever experienced flow – the state where 'aha' moments seem to flow through you continuously – your brain waves are usually in the transition phase from alpha to theta waves, the same as in REM sleep.

I often experience this in the shower and during meditation. Most of my ideas arise in the shower while standing under running drinking water like a modern-day Marie Antoinette. I've had small water-resistant notepads in my shower for years in which I write all my fantasies, which is how I came up with the idea for this book. When I do four phase meditation, which I learned from my mentor Jesse Elder, I come up with new insights and answers for my life and work. It's not a esoteric, vague or highly spiritual technique but a simple way to train your mind to make connections other than the obvious. Anyone can learn it.

Check **www.marijevogelzang.nl/lickit** and learn how to apply four phase meditation yourself.

For example, before my mediation or shower session starts, I ask myself: 'What if... I write a book about food and the creative process?'

I then write: 'I can have a lot of fun because this is exactly where my interests lie: the creative thinking process and food. I can reach people who normally don't see my installations. I can get people to do things themselves so everyone can experience creative thinking with food in their own life. I can use the book to get people to experience the joy and magic of food because I know that many people like food but also see it as a problem. I can interview interesting people and learn new things. I can set up an Instagram account for people to share their results of this book's challenges. I can share my wonderment with food so that maybe people pay more attention and give love to their food.'

And my list goes on and on.

My design process starts with finding a different perspective.

As you can see, some of my motivations are selfish. The chance of a project succeeding is much greater when you enjoy it. More fun creates more attention and more involvement. When faced with a setback, it's easier to find the perseverance to move on. My answer to the what-if question gives my head the opportunity and space to develop a vision. Only then is it time for the how and why questions. And if you get stuck in a rut, then go back to 'what if...?' Alternatively, you could go for a walk or meditate to subdue the beta waves.

For me, this is the start of the design process. Many people think of design as making something beautiful. The aesthetic dimension is indeed essential. I consider it as a means of communication, just like language. You can learn a language, but ultimately it depends on what you want to say with it. My design process starts with finding another perspective so that you can see something new or different in the things already there. Start with the vision and then choose the language with which you want to express the vision.

What if... we treated food as if our lives depended on it?

challenge

write your own 'what if' story

Creating what-if questions is an interesting exercise even if you are not a designer. It will challenge your brain to think differently. Doing so keeps your brain flexible and helps you find less obvious solutions in other situations.

Take your time for this challenge. Make sure you can sit undisturbed, put on some good music and pour yourself a nice drink.

step 1

Start by thinking up some what-if questions related to food. Take an inquisitive look around your head.
For example: **What if sugar had a blue-black colour, so food with more sugar is greyer than food without sugar?**

Try to be curious and complete the list below. Don't think about 'how' or 'why' just yet.

step 2

From the formulated questions, choose the one you found the most challenging. Then describe what life would be like if your idea were a reality.

What if...? (insert your idea here)

What would we eat then?

Who would be involved?

What would change?

What would be the unexpected side effects?

How would it change our perception of food?

What else can you say about this?

I live
to die

death

I once posted a photo on Instagram of two roast chickens surrounded by roasted rosemary potatoes. I had stuffed them under the skin with crushed thyme and lemon. The skin was baked crispy golden brown, the inside visibly juicy. Soon the hearts and reactions poured in. 'Yummy!' 'Enjoy your meal,' 'Do you have the recipe for me?' a little later, I posted a picture of the same two chickens from when I had just slaughtered them. They hung upside down to drain, eyes red with blood and limp like rag dolls. The reactions were equally fast but with far fewer hearts. Most people were shocked and even distraught. One person was downright angry. How dare I kill chickens! I was a murderer.

Cooking is murder.
We use sharp weapons to do the chopping and cutting in the kitchen. There is also killing with boiling water, hot oil and pureeing. Cooking involves fire or icy, painful cold. This activity is even more intense in restaurant kitchens with their hi-speed shouting, scorching, plucking, whipping and controlled rotting, otherwise known as fermentation. Death is no wallflower here but thrives as it crawls over chopping blocks and spills out of pans and refrigerators. Everything that ever lived, grew, bloomed, frolicked or thrashed is now lifeless and ready to be eaten. Time passes,

and life withers, decays and perishes. Though food is life for us, it is inevitably death for another. Indeed, death gives life.

Food is death.
Food is sex.
Food is transience.

As a six-year-old boy, artist Salvador Dalí wanted to become a chef. His fascination for food never waned. Together with his wife and muse Gala, he hosted fabulously opulent dinners. While he offered up sumptuous dishes full of exotic food, wild animals would roam the space. The eroticism and aggression of the luxurious setting were not only tangible but also digestible. The cookbook 'Les dîners de Gala', which Dalí published in 1973, shows the interplay between the dishes and their matching paintings. The morbid and paranoid-surreal dishes are interspersed with images steeped in horniness. There are fowl with twisted skulls, lobsters piled high on a mound of butchered people, and a woman whose severed arms serve as a fountain with blood pouring out like champagne. Though these images are intentionally brazen, they are perhaps more sincere than the polished, sterile depictions found in regular cookbooks. Food is death. Food is sex. Food is transience. Seeing and realising this puts you back in your place.

I was a bit apprehensive about killing and slaughtering a chicken. The first time I did it, I read up on it extensively and mentally prepared myself. I killed firmly with a knife. Not particularly clever, because everything was covered in blood afterwards, and I didn't realise the chickens would convulse for so long. I hung them from an old paint ladder as they quivered to and fro, creating a gory Jackson Pollock on the white fence. After washing my hands inside, I came back outside to find one of the chickens had swung off and was in a pool of blood on the ground. 'To run like a headless chicken' is an aphorism for a reason. The second time I slaughtered chickens was as part of a project. I enlisted the help of Michael Moerman from Stadskip (City Chicken), an organisation that helps people keep chickens in the city sustainably. In the workshop 'Humane Slaughter', I learned to break a chicken's neck with my hands so that it dies immediately and calmly. No knives, so no bloodbath. After the chicken has convulsed while you hold it firmly, you then hang it upside down. The blood then flows to the crop, a pouch under the bird's head. To make plucking easier, you dip the chicken briefly in a large pan of boiling water to make the feathers come off more easily. This process also clots the blood in the head, allowing you to decapitate the chicken cleanly. This method of slaughter requires a very physical relationship between the butcher and the chicken. You hold it, close to your stomach. You focus. You feel the life in the animal connects to the life in you. You break the neck without asking. The knife won't do it for you. You do it yourself, using your own strength.

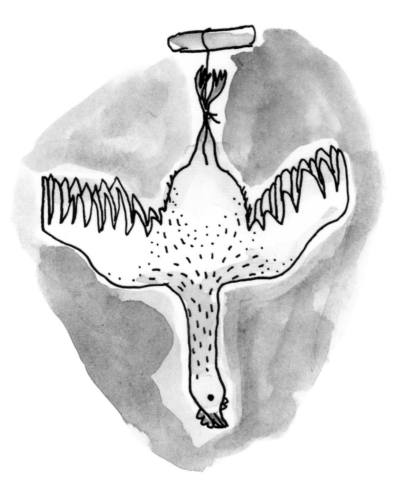

Suddenly it's no longer an animal. You have a piece of meat in your hands.

Somehow this process reminded me of giving birth, but the other way around. It filled me with respect, humility and a strange awareness of how we take lives on a large scale without consent. The chickens hung in a row like white angels, their wings slightly spread apart as if they had just departed. The light shone through their feathers and gave them a soft and untroubled appearance. The animal you dip in the boiling water stinks. The water enhances the odour, and the clean white feathers turn yellowish. The carcasses you pluck are like heavy dolls. They are not yet stiff and hang over your knees. Now they are bald. You slide your hand inside the chicken and feel the warmth. It doesn't feel dead yet. Then you pull out the entrails. Fascinating shapes and colours lie in your hand. If you cut incorrectly, the smell will make you gag. You still see a dead animal. Guts out, head off, and legs too. Suddenly it is no longer an animal. You have a piece of meat in your hands, and your stomach rumbles as your appetite stirs. For chicken.

This transformation from chicken to meat demonstrates the difference in how we talk about animals and meat. We eat 'beef' and 'pork' and not 'cow' and 'pig'. We eat 'brisket' and 'hams' instead of the 'chest' and 'buttocks'. My father is a meat lover, but he hates bones. If there are any on his plate, he moans like a teenager at a campsite with no Wi-Fi. He knows this is hypocritical, but it ruins his appetite to think about the actual animal.

What if you had to slaughter every animal yourself before you could eat it? That you get permission to eat meat only after killing it? That it is added to your 'slaughter passport'? This is what friends Daniël Gravemajer, David de Jong and Tim Stet asked themselves. They decided to observe three rules when eating meat:

1. **look the animal in the eye,**
2. **kill the animal, and**
3. **eat something from that animal.**

Only then did they permit themselves to eat meat. They slaughtered various animals, from lamb to cow and from salmon to pig. They portrayed their personal experiences with arresting honesty in their beautiful book 'Slaughter Passport', which has a metal knife in the cover and pages that you have to slit open. You see the three friends in the slaughterhouse looking dirty with a dead duck in hand. You see them nauseous on a fishing boat. My seven-year-old daughter cuts open several pages and sees a bloody cow hanging with its head in a bucket. 'What animal cruelty!' she yells, taking a bite of her sausage. 'Why do they do that?' The three friends conclude that killing itself isn't even that difficult, an insight that causes them some remorse. Is it wrong that they can do this so easily? They conclude that fish are probably killed more inhumanely than other animals. Their journey results in more respect for meat, butchers, and the other professionals involved. You waste nothing when you do the slaughtering yourself.

Adelaide Lala Tam made a paperclip vending machine. The machine has a video screen, underneath which is a slot for a five euro cent coin and a dispensing compartment. Put a coin in the slot and a video starts playing. It begins by showing a large brass paper clip being pulled apart slowly. The brass wire is coiled, and the moment the brass liquefies, you realise the hypnotic video is playing backwards, and you are going back in time. The liquid metal forms back into a bullet. The bullet of a stun gun. The kind that launches a pin into a cow's head at slaughter.

Then you see the cow. The camera shows a close-up of its beautiful dark brown eyes and soft, caramel-coloured hair. The cow looks to the side, the stun gun pressed to its head. As the pin discharges with a loud bang, the screen goes black. A small package containing a brass paper clip simultaneously falls into the vending machine's dispensing compartment. It looks and feels slightly thicker than a regular paper clip. It weighs 0.9 grams, the same as the bullet casing.

Why a paper clip?
When Adelaide started her graduation project, she first wanted to keep and slaughter a cow herself, but this is a difficult thing to do in a student room in Eindhoven. She had already witnessed the slaughter of a cow in Indonesia. The whole village was involved. The blood coloured the ground deep-red. She shared her images of the experience, which had made a lasting impression. So much so that she went to Dutch slaughterhouses to see how the beautiful cattle were slaughtered. Nothing was thrown away, and every part of the animal had a destination. The only waste from the slaughter was the bullet casings, which Adelaide started collecting. She holds out a large bunch of casings in her hand when I speak to her just before her graduation. 'Each shell represents the life of one cow,' she says, looking at me. Adelaide loves beef. 'If you see how cheap beef is and how the supermarkets are full of it as if it is nothing, you lose connection with the impressiveness of a cow. This reduces these majestic animals to an anonymous commodity. Like a paper clip.' I hold the paperclip and look at it. This is no ordinary paper clip. This paper clip symbolises the life of one cow. I close my hand and cherish it.

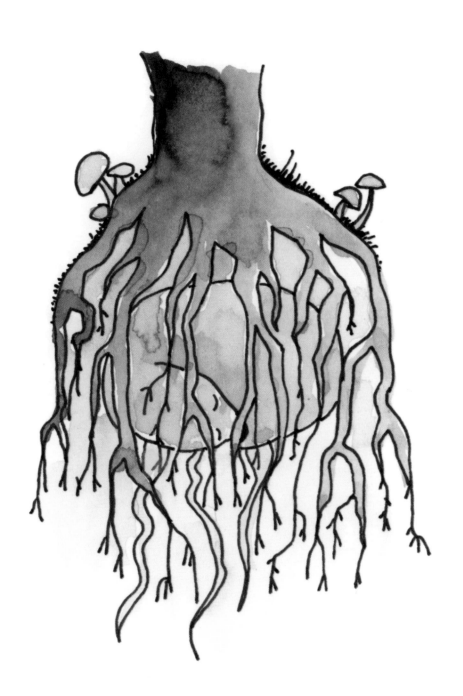

challenge

plan your funeral and meal

No, dear reader, this challenge will not ask you to slaughter an animal. I do not want an unprepared slaughter on my conscience. If you, as a meat-eater, would like to slaughter an animal, then ask for help or guidance from someone who knows how to do it. At least this way, you will do it as efficiently and painlessly as possible. This challenge is not about causing death, but it is about death. Your own death.

We eat to avoid dying. However, food doesn't stop us from dying. Eventually, you will die. But just as slaughterhouses are tucked away out of sight, and many people do not see how animals are slaughtered, we are also moving cemeteries further and further outside the city. Thus, we are confronted less and less with death.

Many cultures have elaborate rituals that accompany a funeral. There are special dishes that are only eaten when someone dies. For example, at a Chinese funeral, you sometimes receive sweets in an envelope to soften the bitterness of loss. In Russia, people eat kollyva, a ceremonial dish made of wheat grains that symbolises the cycle of life. In Korea, people eat yukgaejang, a spicy beef soup whose chilli pepper is said to protect guests from ghosts. In the Netherlands, where I come from, we hardly ever have elaborate food at funerals. We often joke about the pitiful cup of coffee with a slice of cake that is usually served at Dutch funerals.

As a student, I made a white funeral meal as an alternative for those unfortunate Dutch people without a good food culture. I used the colour white because this is the colour that represents death in some cultures. In Europe, it is more commonly black, but I think white is more appropriate. I used naturally white ingredients and combined them in a simple way. It was served on specially made white crockery on a white table, with everyone wearing white clothing. The whole experience had a sense of serenity. And it invited guests to a similarly serene act of contemplation. You ate with your hands so that, in your sorrow, you consciously made contact with your senses. Coincidentally, the taste palette of white food is appropriate for a funeral. Rice, white bread and white vegetables, such as cauliflower and bean sprouts, all have a very subtle flavour. In addition, there are bitter and also sharp flavours, such as chicory, goat cheese and garlic. Together they form a flavour composition that is appropriately symbolic of death.

Nowadays, increasingly fewer people arrange their funeral according to their cultural tradition. What would you like for your farewell after you have passed away? Would you like a big party, like in New Orleans, where high-ranking members of society get a jazz funeral? They are brought to the cemetery in a procession accompanied by jazz music. Or would you like an intimate picnic on a mountain where your friends will scatter your ashes if the wind is right? Think about what you would like and describe below what should happen when 'your moment' arrives. If you come up with something special, it is a pity that you cannot be there yourself. Therefore, you might consider a dress rehearsal.

Share your funeral meal on instagram: **@lickit.book**

ask:

Who should attend?

Where will it take place?

What will the guests drink?

What will the guests eat?

What will the food look like?

Will you use tableware? If so, which?

Is a ritual performed while eating? If so, what will it be?

Are there more things happening?

Do the guests get a memento from you to take home?

good

Sustainability is like a grubby white shirt with yellow armpit stains worn by an overweight, white, Netflix-watching man: it's practical and feels good, but it's not sexy. A passion killer, to be more precise.

Organic lettuce uses more soil and water than lettuce grown in hyper-controlled greenhouses with purple light. Which do you choose? Animal-friendly eggs often give the chicken more space but are less sustainable. Sustainable eggs are often less friendly to the chicken. Which do you choose? In the winter, you can buy locally produced greenhouse tomatoes in the Netherlands. But if you absolutely want tomatoes in the winter, buying them from Morocco or Spain is more sustainable. Which do you choose? Cows cause emissions, but one litre of cow's milk is eight times more nutritious than a litre of oat milk. Per litre, oat milk requires more agricultural land than cow's milk. Cows, in turn, make that milk from grass that grows on land that cannot grow oats or wheat. Which do you choose?

Don't ask me, because I have no idea.
What I know is that these four examples are the tip of the proverbial iceberg. Knowing which food

choice is the most sustainable is a remarkably complex issue and presents unseen hazards. You can devote all your time trying to make the best possible decision, but the outcome will likely be that you go out of your mind or, at the very least, get a pounding headache. If you know what the best choice is for one product, this does not mean the same goes for the next product. Some apps and websites can help you choose a product by showing whether it is better for animals, people or land. However, you will often end up short-changing one of the three. Something good for the land might not be good for the animal or the worker.

Now and then, my interest in sustainability intensifies. I was a member of Slow Food for a long time, I am a member of a local organic shop, and I support farmers' initiatives when my self-employed status affords me the disposable income to do so. Then, after a few weeks of paying close attention to what I buy, other things will catch my attention. These are things that make me happier and give me energy, such as drawing moustaches and eyebrows on babies, taking a long shower and writing on my waterproof notepads, or making nice big porcelain cups for a cappuccino (because the big cups in shops are often so ugly). Large, thinly moulded cups into which you can dollop a generous blob of creamy foam without making a mess. And when I've made such a cup, I don't want coffee with oat milk. I like whole milk from Jersey cows because that's what I enjoy the most. Making ceramics is fun, but do you know how much energy it takes to fire a kiln? And all those raw materials have to come from somewhere. Shame on me!
I spend so much time finding the right apples that are as climate-neutral as possible, but I use all kinds of additional energy for my ceramic kiln. – not to mention that shower. And I fly around the world to give lectures and make installations. The demise of humanity hangs around my neck like a fluffy bunny-eared sloth, and if I'm not careful, it will weigh increasingly heavily on my shoulders.

We want to protect 'nature', but what that is exactly is not entirely clear.

Everyone understands that increasing sustainability makes the world a better place. The food system is one of the best places to start to achieve the most significant impact. What we eat daily has a massive effect on the state of the world. But what sustainability is or entails is not always clear. I started working with food partly because I didn't feel like contributing to the colourful waste mountain of stuff that many designers make. The market is flooded with products and things that go out of style, wear out and that you can't repair yourself. 'At least food is eaten,' I thought, feeling wonderfully superior. But, people have to eat daily, and food production generates considerable waste and pollution. You buy bread much more often than new sneakers.

Perhaps we should first look at the concept of 'sustainability'. Essentially, it means minimising the burden on the ecosystem and improving that ecosystem. I say ecosystem here, but that doesn't clarify which ecosystem to protect. The rainforest ecosystem? The ecosystem under your armpits or in your gut? The ecosystem between humans and animals? And therein lies the problem: we want to protect something vague. We want to protect 'nature', but what that is exactly is not entirely clear. We want insects in the garden but shudder at cockroaches in our house. And we don't want humankind to become extinct, which, frankly, would be the boon nature needs. 'Here you are, Nature. For your birthday, you will receive COVID-22, a virus that threatens human existence and comes in special, limited-edition packaging. Enjoy your gift!'

at least I'm a vegetarian.

As such, we seek a balance between humankind and nature. I, Marije, am a human. But I am not humankind. And what is nature? If I am a human being, am I not also part of nature? And if so, why am I polluting my environment? You may be saying it's the fault of industry, but industry is made and driven by people. Are those 'non-natural' people different from the 'natural' human? The 'natural' human versus the 'industrial' human'? And if humankind created industry, what can I, a seemingly insignificant and tiny individual, do about this? The sustainability problem feels so overwhelming. This is what makes it an unsustainable issue. You know that you want to be a good person and separate your waste, but deep down, do you really want to do this chore. And, does your modest contribution make sense given the bigger picture? If I fire up my ceramic kiln, what's the point of eating that local organic apple that also happens to be an endangered variety? The cumulative effect of your powerlessness makes you feel stressed.

Do you know what is not sustainable? Stress.
Stress is simply a trigger mechanism for your body. It helps when, for example, you are attacked by a lion or, more likely, are about to be robbed by a savage grandmother on steroids. But stress caused by worrying about catching the bus, saying something wrong, or the world is coming to an end isn'tsustainable. You might think stressing out about our increasingly polluted world is good because it will spur you into action. This seems logical until you consider that people who constantly feel stressed get sick. Consequently, they make bad decisions because they are stressed. You can eat the most sustainable apples and stop eating meat, but you will remain constantly stressed if your mind is preoccupied with so many other matters. If you feel like you have to dash around all day – to work, to the supermarket, to day care to pick up your kids, home to clean and pay your bills – how much capacity does your mind have for sustainable deeds?

Help! Do I have to do all this and be sustainable as well? Instead of stress, a sense of urgency is healthier: a controlled and clear sense of urgency and a superhero-like focus. A stressed person tends to act on impulse. You can write a book about the sustainability of oat milk compared to cow's milk, but what if all your knowledge doesn't come across? Perhaps the person for whom it was written rushes around anxiously, trying to find some clarity. This person will obediently buy oat milk, but when switching back to cow's milk (it tasted better anyway), guilt and stress set in because it's the 'wrong' choice. Welcome to the swamp of sustainability and virtue! Here, you are slowly ensnared by monsters in grubby shirts that pull you down from the depths.

Is our brain constantly looking for something to stress about?

When I work with food companies and governmental organisations, they often say that consumers should be given more knowledge about food and that there should be more 'transparency in the chain', which is definitely true. Indeed, knowing more about food leads to different choices, and understanding where things come from is valuable.

But what does the life of the eater look like? Do consumers have the time, space and peace of mind to absorb and act upon all the knowledge that's increasingly becoming available to them? The food industry doesn't think it's such a calamity that there are so many stressed people. They are happy to lend a hand with ready-made meals, for example, or small doses of food you can eat at the wheel or desk. 'No problem. When people are stressed, we have to make things easier for them, right?' But is it the food industry's responsibility to relieve people of their stress? I don't think so. However, the industry can help people to make more sustainable choices by making these decisions for them in advance. Perhaps that responsibility also lies with the government or the media. Whatever the answer is, the fact is you can do something about it right now.

Ultimately, only you can do something about your stress. This might seem impossible to you now because, for example, how can you change your study pressure? However, isn't it strange that the number of stressed people grows as we increasingly surround ourselves with luxury and comfort? Indeed people have never had it so comfortable. Could it be that our brain is constantly seeking stress? Quitting your studies offers acute stress relief; however, your brain then looks very effectively for other sources of stress. Do you worry about the pressure of studying? But then, without study pressure, you worry about something else. You have taught your brain to be a worrying brain.

Rational and irrational stress are different. Rational stress is functional: your house is on fire, so you run outside. You are rightly in a state of alarm and take action in a life-threatening situation! Irrational stress is when you are not in a life-threatening situation, but it affects your body as if you are. You can feel irrational stress when you are worrying. You worry about the climate or that your children are not eating vegetables. It's irrational stress because you are worried about something that might happen, but you don't have to trigger the fight or flight response and go into a state of panic. It is nice to assign someone or something to be responsible for your stress, but you make yourself powerless by thinking, 'I will only feel good if this changes.' The fact is that you can feel good even if many things worry you. Take responsibility for how you feel because apart from your impending bankruptcy or divorce, you can feel wonder and gratitude for everything right in your life. This isn't always easy and requires practise, but it makes everything more straightforward and more enjoyable: you will always be with you, and thus the same goes for this insight.

Don't confuse stress with focus.
Focus can arise from stress. That's why people sometimes think they need pressure to focus. But focus does not exist in the past or the future. It only exists in the present and can help you resolve things. Worrying about the past or the future (thus old or potential stress) hinders focus. Flow and focus are essential for delivering creative work, but chronic stress gets in your way because it blocks your brain. Spiritual thinker Eckhart Tolle shows that 'the now' is the only moment in which we live and in which we will always live. Even if you think you are in the future, you are still in the now. You simply cannot be in any other time. Our brains, on the other hand, are always thinking about what happened in the past or what might happen in the future. Hence, you sometimes forget to be in the moment. All this may sound counter-intuitive in terms of sustainability because it is pre-eminently about the future. Yes, but how can that save our world now, Marije? Living in the now gives you some leeway in your life. That's true, but it doesn't mean you never think about the future. From the present, you can observe all past and future times and consciously decide where your focus lies. If you can experience the present as a stress-free moment, you can be yourself, enabling you to make much better decisions.

If you genuinely derive pleasure and satisfaction from your contribution, it won't cost you any effort.

That's all very well, but how do you do this? Many books have been written on the subject – even more than on sustainability. It starts with the awareness that you can relax. So, although we live in a world with climate change, animal cruelty and land degradation, chronic stress does not solve these problems. Chances are you are only making them worse. You, the reader of this book, can start by acknowledging that everything is actually quite okay at this very moment. Maybe you're in debt, and perhaps you're going to die. But at this very moment, you are just sitting quietly, reading this book. You're not about to be beaten up or pounced upon by a hungry, mangy lion. And if you are, the spine of this book has reinforced steel to fight off the attacker! If that's not necessary, you can put this book down for a moment and take a deep breath. Of course, things are going on in your life: what is life without 'things'? This is part of life, and it carries you further. But at this precise moment, everything is pretty good. There is the day and the night. Love exists. Deepen your breathing. You can read, and you can think. Fill the present space and time, as it were, with your presence. Relax. Everything is fine at this moment. Suppose you are comfortable in your skin. In that case, it's easy to separate your waste while singing (or don't make any waste), to eat tasty vegan food, to smell wonderful even though you've not taken a shower, and to leave the heating off so you can wrap yourself in your most beautiful woollen pyjama suit – just because you feel like it. It's not that hard, right? I know a number of people who seem to be able to do this fairly easily and don't understand why everyone does not live this way. I also know many more people for whom this does not work and have absolutely no desire for it.

yes, me too.

Desire. Exactly that.
Sustainable sustainability is doing something you desire rather than what you think you should do. If you genuinely derive pleasure and satisfaction from your contribution, it won't cost you any effort. When you feel good and are not constantly plagued by stress, you feel that you can contribute more clearly to the greater good. If you feel deeply connected with what is alive, using shampoo with microplastics is simply illogical. Pollution feels like licking an ashtray if you genuinely feel in awe of the magic of nature's network. You are part of that network, and the world influences you just as much as you influence the world. When you see the extraordinary

way that plants, animals, insects, fungi and microbes interact, you can't help but marvel. Nature's unfailing aesthetic appeals to everyone, whether the veins of a tree's leaf or light patterns dancing on the water. City dwellers can spend a whole day without touching a living organism. (Except microorganisms, of course; you can't escape those!) You may see some plants in the form of vegetables in the supermarket, but they are only the severed limbs of the flora to which they once belonged. The ready-to-use items from the shop are far removed from the soil in which the plant grew and the stages the plant went through until its harvest. So it isn't easy to feel the magical connection with nature when you don't see it. The saying 'out of sight, out of mind' rings true here. With every courgette you buy, you should get a mini-documentary.

By marvelling and enjoying ourselves now, we may find the motivation for real change.

We live a world of beautiful and natural complexity. It is nothing short of a wonderland. That we have food and clean water at all is a miracle. I know this sounds corny, but let that sink in. It is something for which we should exercise boundless and profound gratitude! David Attenborough, the famous nature documentary maker, understands this acutely and says, 'No one will protect what they don't care about, and no one will care about what they have never experienced.' Sustainable behaviour is currently being stimulated among consumers and companies. Fortunately, our 'sustainable awareness' has grown considerably in the past ten years. Still, when push comes to shove, for many people, this awareness still feels like a burden. It's as if they have to make sacrifices when actually it's about embracing the sheer joy of life. If we are faced with feelings of guilt, we end up in a negative spiral. If we genuinely marvel at and enjoy – in the now – nature's wonder and its edible offerings, then we may find the motivation for real change.

challenge

restore the earth while eating!

Did you know that one of the most significant sustainability issues is the health of agricultural land? The soil in which we grow vegetables, grow crops for our animal feed and graze the animals whose meat and milk we consume is in bad shape. Our earth is becoming exhausted in more and more places. This process can be counteracted with green manures. These are soil-restoring plants, including legumes such as peas, lentils and beans. Is making the soil healthier just a matter of growing and eating more beans? Yes, it is! But do you want to do that?

In 2018, I gave a performance for AXIS gallery in Tokyo called 'The Future in Your Hands'. I had people eat soil-regenerating snacks out of my hand. But why?

Firstly, because I wanted to know what felt like it. Having people eat out of your hand is a very intimate experience, and I was curious what it would be like. It feels funny in your hand, especially when it's a man with a beard or moustache.

Secondly, because you need the confidence to eat out of my hand. Is my hand clean? Is this not crazy? You let animals eat from your hand – but people? However, you need confidence when thinking about a healthy future. We humans are dependent on one another. Distrust fosters alienation and an anonymous culture behind which you can hide. Companies with more rules have more distrust, and their staff take less responsibility. Trust creates connection, cooperation and the feeling of being part of a greater whole.

Thirdly, because you have a healthy future in your hands. The choices you make in your life allow you to steer the ship of the world better. And who knows, you might inspire others.

Sometimes these choices can be small: choosing to feel good, choosing regenerative ingredients that make the soil better rather than polluting and depleting it. Thus you heal the earth while eating. If you ensure the food is tasty and enjoy making it, it becomes truly sustainable. Of course, this is not a cookbook, and I don't know what you like. Hence, I'm giving you a shopping list to choose from. Below is a list of regenerating ingredients and their effect on soil.

- Rye and **buckwheat** put potassium in the soil.
- **Beans, lupine** and **alfalfa** help nitrogen fixation in soil.
- **Samphire** and **sea lavender** are among the few plants that grow on saline and poor soil (thus very sustainable even when there are freshwater shortages).
- **Hemp** (seed) grows on poor soil, can remove heavy metals from the soil and releases more oxygen into the air than trees do.
- **Edible flowers** help insects.
- **Seaweed** does not need farmland, freshwater or fertiliser.
  Ocean algae and seaweed are responsible for seventy per cent of all oxygen in the air.
- **Fungi** and **mushrooms** help a healthy soil. They break down waste and toxins, which in turn nourishes the soil.
- **Nuts** are part of agroforestry: a sustainable growing method.
  The trees put oxygen into the air, and their roots help against erosion.

I also want to share a simple recipe if you have no inspiration and want to save the world while enjoying yourself hedonistically. My friend Merijn Tol writes for Delicious magazine and makes cookbooks about the Arab world. Her recipes connect to people and stories. Merijn cooks the tastiest things from the simplest ingredients. When I visit her, she occasionally runs into her kitchen to turn some simple onions into the most mouth-watering umami bombs. She turns modest ingredients into a table full of abundance with rich flavours and textures. If anyone can help us make regenerative food delicious, it's her!

recipe

Toasted buckwheat and hemp salad with white beans, wildflowers and herbs, roasted hazelnut oil and stir-fried sea lavender with garlic, mushrooms and salty seaweed powder

100 g white beans, soaked or canned (less tasty, but quicker)
200 g buckwheat
200 g hemp
handfuls of edible flowers, herbs
50 g hazelnuts
good wine vinegar
olive oil
300 g mixed mushrooms
150 g sea lavender
3 garlic cloves
crispy seaweed (nori)

Boil the beans in plenty of salted water until tender. Soaked beans take about 30 to 45 minutes to cook – taste regularly. Canned beans do not need cooking, only draining.

Toast (being careful not to burn) the buckwheat and hemp in a frying pan over medium heat for 10 to 12 minutes until nutty.
Finely chop the wildflowers and herbs.
Roast the hazelnuts and purée into a liquid hazelnut oil with salt and olive oil.
Roughly chop the mushrooms and fry until golden brown in some olive oil, sprinkle with salt.
Finely chop the garlic and add to the mushrooms, stir fry for 5 to 8 minutes and add the sea lavender.
Grind the crispy seaweed (nori) into a powder.

Mix the beans with the buckwheat, hemp, herbs, wildflowers, and hazelnut oil and season with vinegar and salt.
Spoon onto a plate with some mushrooms and sea lavender on the side, and sprinkle some seaweed powder over the mushrooms.

Now that you're doing all this, why not try eating out of someone's hand.
Share your experiences on instagram: **@lickit.book**

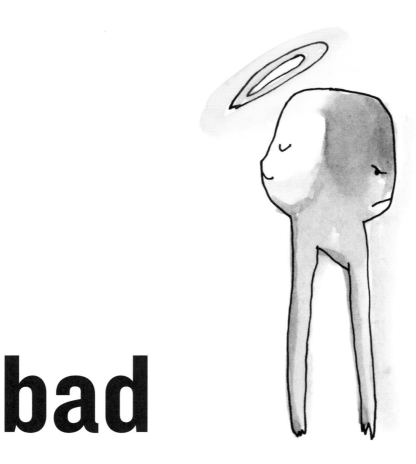

bad

There is non-sustainable sustainability, where you rationally want to do something but don't have the will. And there is sustainable sustainability, where you are happily eager to make sustainable choices. The sustainability paradox is that we are simply human.

Our rational self wants to do good but also desires a little bad. The Chinese philosopher Confucius believed that people are good by nature, but we all have a little bit of mischief and don't have to suppress it. The Jewish principle of 'yetzer hara' has the same premise: everyone has an innate tendency to be a rascal. This isn't necessarily considered wrong: the salt in the soup gives life flavour. However, too much salt ruins the soup.

The human endeavour to live sustainably is, of course, very noble. But the will to do 'the right thing' also precludes a lot of innovative thought and creativity. It has the effect of a creative castration. If you allow yourself to think only about sustainable and correct things, you narrow the scope for experimentation and freethinking, resulting in bland, predictable and unfruitful ideas. Unique insights sometimes emerge when you allow your thinking process to accommodate 'wrong' ideas and thoughts. The fear of being politically, sustainably or ethically incorrect is paralysing. I know students who are so afraid of designing something that might offend that they keep walking down the same well-trodden paths. Fear of pollution makes them afraid to experiment with materials. Fear of confrontation makes them hide behind vague words. That we want to be good people is honourable, but your mind should be a sanctuary for experimentation and unlimited imagination. What you ultimately create in your head and cast into the world is up to you, and you are responsible for it. What is visible is the outcome. But let's also look at the invisible: the process.

By embracing the 'negative', sparkling new ideas can arise.

To allow yourself to think creatively and freely, sometimes you must swim in chaos first. In Greek mythology, first, there was nothing but chaos. From that chaos emerged the Gods, the world and the underworld. Many cultures have their God of chaos, disobedient figures who happily saw the legs off from under someone's chair. Perhaps they are annoying, but in retrospect, sometimes they are good. Just look at your life. What did you learn from the most? From sitting comfortably in your chair or falling off and hoisting yourself back up? Chaos has value because you can only perceive something through contrast. Order exists by the grace of chaos, and beauty is only a quality compared to ugliness. In fact, without insipidness, you simply would not perceive what is tasty. So it is necessary that the other side of the coin is there. By embracing the 'negative', sparkling new ideas can arise. For example, you may condemn the fact Coca-Cola can reach the most remote places in the world where there is no medical help and often no clean water. You may think Coca-Cola is the devil and should be banned. You may also see this as an opportunity, as Simon Berry did, and design clever packaging for transporting medicine that fits snuggly between crated Coca-Cola bottles. Instead of condemning Coca-Cola's granular network, he takes positive advantage of it.

When I made an installation for the Swiss furniture brand Vitra, I thought about the location of the Vitra Design Museum: at the tri-border region of Germany, France and Switzerland. When I spoke to local people, they told me that border residents often identify more with their national culture than people in the centre of the country. Apparently, the border provides an instinctive emotional contrast. Biting into a sandwich for lunch, I imagined organisms whose strength derived from genetic diversity rather than segregation. It was a delicious sandwich too: a French baguette with Swiss cheese bought in a German supermarket.

Food is a reflection of national identity.
Almost every country has its traditional dishes. Practically every country in the Western world has an iconic bread that symbolises the country. What if the three countries had hot sex that bore an adorable bread roll lovechild? What would it taste like? The genes of the loaves would reinforce one another and make a more resilient bread. It would be a bread that could bring

people closer together. I ran with this idea and took an iconic loaf from each country – a German dark pumpernickel bread, an airy French baguette and a sweet Swiss Zopf – and created a bread roll: the bastard bread. They were small and easy to share, tied with string in the middle. The three types of dough were not mixed but baked together as strips in one bread roll. When you took a bite, you could still identify the characteristics of the three types of bread, but you soon tasted how they combined to create an exciting flavour sensation. Master baker Fritz Trefzger and his team from Schopfheim perfected the recipe and baked more than two thousand bastard rolls at Zaha Hadid's Vitra Fire Station. The visitors, who shared and ate the bastard rolls with a tasty curl of fresh butter, spontaneously fell in love with one another. It was a hot night. Nine months later, healthy babies were born with robust and diverse genes.

Suppose you take the shortest route from the problem's definition to its solution (see chapter What if?); chances are you will arrive at a predictable answer. A surprise may await if you allow yourself to wander down some exciting, less brightly lit path. Additionally, judgment will often get in your way. You have to judge what is right, what is allowed, what is not, and who is good

and bad. A judgment is something that many people deem an essential accessory to be worn conspicuously. Particularly in Western Europe, people dare not take to the streets without judgment. Watch some television, and you get the impression that being stridently judgemental is the only way to be taken seriously. And, of course, we judge every day, all day long. Do I find this horrible or nice? Do I like them or not? Do I put on flippers when I go outside, or do I wear shoes? We shape ourselves through judgement and the world around us. 'I don't like friendly, local initiatives and prefer to spend a lot of money at Starbucks.'

Judgment restrains curiosity and thus opportunities for discoveries.

Judgments help us organise our lives (see chapter Crooked) but also inhibit our thinking process. When you judge something, you inhibit your curiosity: the essential ingredient for making discoveries. Have you ever tried not to judge? It's rather difficult. You may also think that what you judge is fixed, such as good taste or kindness. However, history and other cultures demonstrate this is not so. In the Netherlands, for example, telling someone frankly what you think of them – or their ravioli – is considered a virtuous and caring act. Asa, who also worked on this book, is from Taiwan and was surprised to learn this. Such directness seemed rude to her. Anyone who thinks that healthy food should consist of a lot of vegetables should talk to Jopie, who was a teenager in Amsterdam when she experienced the Dutch Famine of 1944–1945. 'Healthy food means butter, meat and tasty biscuits,' she told me when I served her mother's wartime recipe for 'stewed pears' made from sugar beet with beetroot juice.

'Tastes differ' is not an obligatory expression said with a shrug when no one likes your homemade whipped-cream truffles. Tastes are judgments, preferences and opinions. We know they differ, but we still find it annoying when someone has a different viewpoint. You don't get much out of being judgemental, either. The thing or the person you are judging will not go away. In fact, people you judge tend to hold on to their beliefs even more tightly. Judging someone is like poisoning yourself because you will suffer the most.

I know someone who was very irritated by the experience of being at IKEA. He is the only one who suffers as a consequence: IKEA doesn't care. When you judge something as 'bad' or 'stupid', you feel the energy drain from you – energy that you could better spend on developing alternatives! If you can't influence the thing that irks you, you can also decide to be indifferent to it. You might feel awkward and say, 'Yeah, but then it seems I don't care!' But what difference does it make if you can't change it, it makes you suffer, and it wastes your energy? By not caring about it, you don't waste your energy. You might even manage to look neutrally at the thing you judge. It may even arouse your curiosity. You might condemn Starbucks but discover that their business model can work well when applied to a seed bank for heirloom vegetables. Perhaps you will find that you can have an influence. And if you can influence something, care about it with every ounce of your being!

challenge

pitch a bad idea!

Well, this is turning out to be a strange chapter in a book about food and creative thinking. First, it tackled sustainability, then stress and living 'in the now'. When it comes to creative thinking, it's about not judging and embracing 'bad' things. 'I thought I'd bought a book about food,' you stammer disappointedly.

Still, it's fun to see how your food experiences change when you test these ideas in your own life. If you think in more than one direction and replace your judgment with curiosity, will the eating experience also change? Perhaps this feels like an impossible task for you. Some people identify with their sense of judgment. Who are you without your judgment? Remember that children do not judge. Hence, they are not bad people and usually have a more flexible view of the world. It's not about what you think; it's about what you do!

We shall go one step further with this challenge. Not only shall we reserve our judgement, but we shall also spread 'bad' ideas! This challenge is part of my online course, 'Food and Design Dive'. In the online session, we discuss all kinds of designs that are abrasive or intended to make you think. For example, there is Johanna Schmeer's design for bioplastics that, with the aid of synthetic biology, can behave like green leaves on a tree and photosynthesise. She then creates materials for edible substances, such as powder and slime. Then there is Leo Fidjeland and Linnea Våglund's 'Pink Chicken Project' that proposes using CRISPR technology to give all production chickens a dominant gene to make their feathers, bones and eggs pink. Our mass consumption of chicken will leave a pink layer in Earth's rock strata. People in the future will see how we overconsumed in the Anthropocene (the proposed name for the geological epoch dominated by human influence). Ai Hasegawa made a beautiful video of a woman in a thin white dress. She gives birth to a dolphin in a pool, intending to eat this endangered species later. Austin Stewart's virtual reality headset for industrial chickens shows them lush green fields, so they don't spend their lives looking at a sad chicken shed full of sun-deprived animals. Remarkably enough, many of the course's participants consider this art project crude, yet some Russian farmers do this with their cows.

When it comes to food, ethical discussions are never far away – which is a good thing too, because it means we care.

what will you do?

Read the newspaper or search online to find a food story that makes your skin crawl. You can also concoct a news story yourself, such as:
- Due to sustainability concerns, we shall eat all shelter animals.
- We shall abolish half of all parking spaces and turn them into flower beds for bees.
- Special removable stomach bags have been developed that allow you to eat continuously.
- In the interests of sustainability, there are plans for the mandatory consumption of Soylent (a meal replacement drink) once a week.
- Only rich people should eat meat.

Well, I guess they should provoke some strong reactions.
Choose something to which you are vehemently opposed. Share the message in a Whatsapp group, during a dinner with friends or online, and pretend you think it might be a good idea. Ask your friends or colleagues what they think and collect the different opinions.
If the reactions become problematic for you, blame this book and ritually burn it!

Many of my students initially found it daunting to share an idea with which they disagreed. Nevertheless, they were often surprised at the refreshing reactions and insights they received. Sometimes things are not so black and white.

How did this challenge work out for you?
What did it feel like to temporarily adopt a different position?
Did you gain any new insights?
Share your experiences on instagram: **@lickit.book**

smell

We smell like humans. We smell of sweat and other body odours. We smell wild when we don't wash. When we wash, we use soap. We wash away our body's natural odours. Soap makes us smell like lilacs, papaya or lime. Philipp Kolmann made soap for which he used various wild animals: soap from deer, soap from wild boar, and soap from hare. Each soap smelled of a specific animal. After washing with this soap, you are clean, but your skin smells like a wild animal. Do you think that's dirty? If so, why?

I'm allergic to peanuts.
I only found out when I was twenty-one and ate a pack of Wibra meringue biscuits known as 'goats legs' (bokkenpootjes in Dutch). You're probably wondering how seriously you should take me as a food designer if I eat the cheapest brand of biscuits in the Netherlands. Regardless, I started getting an itchy throat after the goat legs. I ate peanut butter and cocktail nuts throughout my childhood, but they didn't bother me until my twenties. Now, every time I eat a peanut, the reaction is more severe. My allergy could develop into something deadly with a bit of bad luck. I avoid peanuts like the plague, which isn't always easy in restaurants. It's a pity because I used to really like peanut butter, and even now, I can vividly recall its taste in my 'mind mouth'.

I wonder if I were to eat peanut butter now, would I have a 'Proustian experience'? The Proust effect, named after the French writer Marcel Proust, is when you smell or taste something that involuntarily reminds you of something you had forgotten. Proust described this experience in his seven-volume novel 'In Search of Lost Time', first published between 1913 and 1927. Would the taste of peanuts evoke 'hidden memories' in me? The other day, I smelled the paws of our sleeping puppy (my boyfriend said puppy paws smell like popcorn) and was transported back to being a six-year-old in the dog basket of Droopy, my parents' puppy. I had found a hidden memory through smell.

I decided to put my questions to the people at IFF, the fragrance and flavour company I once worked with. They make artificial flavours, but could they make artificial peanut butter? Yes, that's possible! They also make ham and cheese potato chips without ham, thus Muslims and vegetarians can eat them. I was going to taste the fake peanut butter and was very excited about the idea. After all these years, I would taste peanuts again! My fake peanut butter came in the form of white chocolate spread with peanut flavour added. I took a small plastic spoonful of 'peanut butter' from the jar. I had to use some force to get it out. This effort reminded me of the nearly empty jars of Aldi peanut butter that my father would help me scoop out the clotted remains. I raised the spoon to my mouth, and the familiar smell greeted me. But instead of being the key to my hidden memories, it unlocked a physical panic. My whole body tensed up now that I faced the ridiculous and dangerous idea of eating peanuts. Sweating, I told myself: 'This is not actual peanuts. It's just a very convincing flavouring.'

I took a bite.
It was indeed how peanut smells and tastes. My body calmed down and seemed slightly confused. The nice lady from IFF had made an extra pot 'to take home'. The memories and fun I had hoped to experience failed to materialise. The physical sense of panic had been too much, and the jar remained unopened in the refrigerator. Though my body could handle the fake peanut butter, my head couldn't.

Smell and taste dance with each other in your body.

IFF mainly produces fragrances for the detergent and cosmetics industry and flavourings for the food industry. The company was split in two, not only as departments but also as a building, with the left side for smell and the right side for taste. Prior to my visit, I had wild fantasies about the possible exciting collaborations between the smell and taste departments. In practice, these worlds turned out to be strictly separated. The reason for this is that many scents are inedible or even poisonous, whereas flavourings should always be edible. In reality, smell and taste dance with each other wherever you experience them in your body. You smell not only through your nostrils (ortho nasal) but also through your oral cavity (retronasal). Up to ninety-five per cent of what we perceive as taste is, in fact, smell. It's common knowledge that you can taste less when you have a cold. But if you smell different things while eating, that also affects what you taste. If you cut an apple with a knife you used for cutting garlic, you will immediately perceive the smell in your mouth. I find this very annoying! And eating next to a lady or gentleman wearing a pungent fragrance gives a different taste than eating next to a dog that has just farted.

Something that tastes like freshly mown grass – but isn't – can be quite tasty.

Back to the smell and flavour business. The interplay between smell and taste is exciting because it lets us 'taste' things that are actually inedible or even poisonous. Some substances smell lovely but are inedible. The scent of freshly mown grass, for example, evokes memories of summer picnics (while for lawns, it must be a traumatic aroma because it smells like decapitated grass), but we can't digest grass, so we don't eat it. If only something tasted like freshly mown grass, maybe that would be rather tasty. The same goes for the smell of tomato leaf, which also reminds us of summer. Tomatoes are part of the nightshade family, as are potatoes and aubergines, but these plants' foliage is poisonous, so you can't eat the leaves. However, what if you only use the scent as a flavour?

And how about the smell of wood, leather or hay? If ninety-five per cent of what we taste is actually smell, we might as well add the scent of uneatable things to our flavour palette. So, we put this idea to the test. One outcome of the collaboration with IFF was cutlery impregnated with edible scents of cut grass, cedarwood, hay and tomato leaves. We made exciting combinations of aroma and flavour for this cutlery. For a while at Proef, my former restaurant in Amsterdam, we served cotton candy with a mown grass or cedar flavour. You don't need access to a laboratory to experiment with the smell of inedible ingredients. You can also just use the scent. Rub one hand (not your fingertips!) with tomato leaf, and then eat something with that hand.

Smell is terribly important but invisible in our daily life. Is this why we hardly use it actively or consciously? Besides preparing food, we do shockingly little with smell. We will sniff a glass of wine and eagerly inhale the aroma of apple pie, but these scents are as a result of something. When do we actively add fragrance? Nobody perfumes my pancake when I come to visit. You would think this has always been the case, but nothing could be further from the truth. As art historian Caro Verbeek tells me: 'In classical antiquity, people used edible perfumes between meals. The walls were perfumed with saffron at festive banquets, the napkins impregnated with lavender, and the tables smeared with mint. In any case, people lived in a much richer olfactory world than we do now in our sterile homes with flushing toilets and extractor hoods. Many of those past practices aimed to disguise the whiff of rotten food or waste. But scent was also used as an experience in itself. Nice fragrances were more noticeable and sometimes considered sacred.' Imagine yourself with a garland of sweet-smelling roses on your head while simultaneously eating a dish with roses: you would be filled and enveloped with roses inside and out.

'In classical antiquity, people used edible perfumes between meals.'

Nowadays, some fine dining restaurants serve edible perfume. At the Mediamatic institute in Amsterdam, Caro Verbeek has initiated a fragrance programme called 'Odorama' and the 'Neo Futurist Dinners' series of food events. For many years, Chandler Burr, who was The New York Times' longstanding 'scent critic', organised scent dinners inspired by well-known perfumes based on edible ingredients. When I met him years ago in New York, he told me what fascinates him about smell. 'You have seen all the colours you can see in your life and all the tones you can hear too. But new smells will reveal themselves to you throughout your life.' Despite the increased attention to olfactory art and the supermarkets that tempt you with the aroma of freshly baked bread, smell is hardly used in everyday food in the western world. We garnish our food with edible decoration but rarely with fragrance decoration. We buy beautiful coloured napkins and dust off our most beautiful crockery for dinner with friends, but we do not make conscious olfactory choices. Food simply smells like it smells. But we put scented candles in the toilet. And yet fragrances can immediately arouse memories of bygone times – and that doesn't make you fat!

As an art historian, Caro is interested in the art historical role of smell and wrote her PhD on the importance of scent in Futurism. 'One reason scent is hard to research in history is that it is so fleeting, so there isn't much of it left. Yet there are enough clues in texts, artefacts and material remnants to reconstruct the olfactory part of history. Another reason is that the "higher" senses, such as sight and, to a somewhat lesser extent, hearing, have traditionally been at the top of the classical philosophical classification. They were considered more important than the "lower" senses such as touch, taste and smell.' You can still see this in art today. Most people only think of the visual arts when they think of 'art'. Music often comes next. Haptic art is far less common, and taste or smell art is relatively rare. This is why people often think that I only make food look 'beautiful' as a designer: they only consider the visible part. But why should art be exclusively visual?

As an art historian, Caro is interested in the art historical role of smell and wrote her PhD on the importance of scent in Futurism. 'One reason scent is hard to research in history is that it is so fleeting, so there isn't much of it left. Yet there are enough clues in texts, artefacts and material remnants to reconstruct the olfactory part of history. Another reason is that the "higher" senses, such as sight and, to a somewhat lesser extent, hearing, have traditionally been at the top of the classical philosophical classification. They were considered more important than the "lower" senses such as touch, taste and smell.' You can still see this in art today. Most people only think of the visual arts when they think of 'art'. Music often comes next. Haptic art is far less common, and taste or smell art is relatively rare. This is why people often think that I only make food look 'beautiful' as a designer: they only consider the visible part. But why should art be exclusively visual?

Odorphobia is the fear that odours may spread disease.

Caro is particularly fascinated by the vital role scent has played throughout history in both art and social life. 'I am interested in showing this rich history. Around 1880, the Symbolists, for example, used scent to create a harmonious experience. They might diffuse the scent of irises during performances and simultaneously display the letter 'i' in front of an orange projection. Or the musical note 're' might sound as the scent of violets took over the space. The aim was to create well-balanced compositions in which the senses work together. Even earlier, from classical antiquity to the seventeenth century, it was common to accompany theatrical performances with scents. However, this ceased between the late eighteenth and nineteenth centuries due to Odorphobia: the fear that odours may spread disease.

Futurism, an art movement that emerged in the 1910s, used smell, taste and food as art. The Futurists did this not for the sake of a pleasant experience but inspired by industrialisation, aerodynamics and innovation. They also saw food as a medium for their 'Gesamtkunstwerk', or 'syn-

thesis of the arts', where you could experience different art disciplines simultaneously. They aimed to experience life through all the senses simultaneously. But, how do you experience such a thing? Well, for example, you might have felt a 'tactile poem' made of velvet, sandpaper and silk with your left while your right hand brought a bite of olives, artichoke and citrus to the mouth. In combination with music by Bach, the sound of aircraft engines added to this experience, which might have been accompanied by the fragrant smell of carnations.

Filippo Tomasso Marinetti is the Italian founder of Futurism and published 'The Futurist Cookbook' in 1932. It was both a manifesto and a collection of theatrical recipes. One of his statements was that pasta was bad. It had to be banned because it would make you tired, lazy and fat. As you can imagine, this did not go down well in Italy at the time. The Futurists had a political agenda and fascist leanings. They idealised strong, virile men who embraced the future through technology and were contemptuous of the bourgeoisie, with their well-tended gardens, lives, dishes and smells. They also expressed this through their art. The scents they used for their 'dining performances' were carefully chosen. For example, they used aerosol (as a reference to aviation) and eau de cologne, which probably makes you think of your grandmother. However, in the 1930s, this fragrance was associated with war. It was initially used as a disinfectant for minor wounds. But during the First World War, soldiers took it with them and sprinkled it on a hand-kerchief to smell the scent of home. This 'scent of home' was made from Italian ingredients and originally created in 1709 by an Italian hairdresser who took it to Germany. There it became known as Kölnisch Wasser 4711 and later eau de cologne. Cologne also means 'colony' in Italian. The Futurists embraced war, stench and nationalism and used eau de cologne to rinse their eating utensils, as was done during the war. Consequently, the food was lightly perfumed. Marinetti used eau de cologne in several of his book's recipes, including as an ingredient in coffee.

'What I find remarkable is that smell is hugely subjective,' says Caro. 'Smells we liked at a certain time in history, we later found repulsive and vice versa.' She tells of the sweet smell from the mouth of Saint Teresa d'Avila in the sixteenth century. Pilgrims described this fragrance as heavenly. According to Teresa's gardener, she smelled sweeter than orange blossoms and roses. A sweet fragrance was rare in those days and was considered sacred and a sign of purity of soul. The scientific explanation for Teresa's scent is that she probably had diabetes, which she developed from fasting. One person's holy fragrance is another's odour of disease. The smell is a bit like acetone, according to Caro.

Smell is thus not objectively nice or unpleasant.
There are only a few scents that instinctively we immediately detest. These include certain moulds and the smell of decomposition. Furthermore, our experiences and environment determine our 'smell preferences'. According to Caro, these depend entirely on the context. Psychologist Rachel Herz once placed test subjects in a brain scanner and asked them to smell an odour produced by bacteria. While smelling, she told the test participants that the odour came from dirty sports socks. The resulting brain scans showed a reaction from the part of the brain associated with aversion. She used the same smell with another group of test subjects but told them the odour came from tasty French cheeses. This time, the part of the brain linked to pleasure lit up. The results of this test clearly demonstrate the impossibility of objective odour perception. Our opinions about something influence whether we think it smells nice or unpleasant. Hence our strong response to smell even has a measurable physical effect!

What if we hugged our children from an early age surrounded by the smell of Brussels sprouts?

challenge

tomato vine pairing

Sometimes aroma is not very present when we eat. It is there, but we prefer to associate food with the tongue more than the nose. To fully experience and activate your nose, the essential component, or at least the catalyst, must be your sense of smell. We can do this using our favourite fruit: the tomato.

For this challenge, we shall focus on the tomato vines. Though inedible, a tomato's vines contribute significantly to the plant's unique smell. When smelled together with other ingredients, the vines can bring the nose unexpected joy and allow it to become more : familiar with 'eating'. Let's find out what these pairings are and discover new aroma combinations!

instructions:

You will need a sprig of tomato vines. If you don't have access to fresh tomatoes, you can buy them in the supermarket but make sure their vines are still attached.
Our pairing 'starter kit' consists of the following ingredients, so make sure you also get them while on your tomato shopping trip:

1 cucumber
250 g strawberries
1 lime,
1 tin of sweetcorn or 1 cob cooked and separated
1 bar of chocolate
250 ml double cream (it should be liquid, not whipped or clotted)
0.5–1 litre coconut water
1 pack of mushrooms (preferably button or oyster mushroom)

It is not necessary to buy all of the ingredients above, especially if they are unavailable or you have allergies.

You will need a large cutting board.

Remove the vines from the tomatoes.
Put the vines in a dish or container. Store the tomatoes away.
Cut the cucumber, strawberries and lime into slices.
Put the sweetcorn and chocolate into separate dishes.
Pour the cream and coconut water into separate cups.

We shall fry the mushrooms just before serving because you will best experience their aroma when they are hot and steaming.

Place the prepared ingredients (except the mushrooms) and the tomato vines on your cutting board. Gather your 'tasters' around the table. When everyone is seated, fry the mushrooms in a pan with a bit of oil until the mushrooms are cooked and aromatic. Put them in a dish and bring them to the table. Now everyone must be quick.

Use one hand to pick a sprig from the tomato vine and rub it into your fingers.
Pick up a piece of mushroom with your other hand.
Bring both ingredients to your nose and smell the two aromas together, one in each nostril. The distance between your nostrils and the two components is crucial for a good smelling experience. If the vine overpowers the smell of the other ingredient, move it further away, and vice versa. Soon, you will find the proper distance between the ingredients and your nose.

Now try pairing the tomato vine with the other components.

The chocolate and cream have an extra step. After smelling these ingredients in combination with the tomato vine, take a sip of cream or a bite of chocolate and then immediately smell the vine again. Does the smell change? You can also try this extra step with the other ingredients.

If the tomato vine loses its smell, take a new one and work the aroma into your fingers again.

Now that you have mastered the technique, try other aroma combinations that you think would smell good with tomato vines. How about melons or chickpeas? You could also try soy sauce or kiwi fruit. Be experimental!
Share your findings on instagram: **@lickit.book**

Do I have a soul?

next nature

Suppose you leave your phone (which is now probably in your pocket or next to you) at home. It probably feels like you're missing a limb, right? You feel incomplete. You might even go back to get it because you miss it every time you want to take a quick photo or send a message. Likewise, your fingers want to type and swipe but can't. It's like phantom pain after an amputation.

All of which is quite bizarre. Especially when you consider that not so long ago, we thought we didn't need mobile phones. They were unnecessary gadgets – a novelty for impatient people. Sometimes, I jokingly tell students that when, around 1998, I discovered something special like sushi, I would go to the library in Eindhoven and borrow all the books on Japanese cooking. I couldn't look it up 'online'. To the students, it's as if I'm from prehistoric times because they can't imagine life without online information. Google has become a natural resource and an undeniable 'life partner'.

'Our idea of nature is that it is born or grown but not human-made.'

Artist-philosopher Koert van Mensvoort calls our unfolding relationship with technology 'Next Nature'. It describes a condition where something does not seem natural, yet it is increasingly natural to us and sometimes even almost physical and, therefore, biological. Many people say they want to eat 'natural', but what exactly is natural? 'Our traditional idea of nature is that it is born or grown but not human-made. Nowadays, it may be interesting and necessary to rethink our idea of nature,' says Koert. Let's consider this in the context of food. The technology of cooking food allows us to digest food outside our bodies because the process starts in the pan. We would say that cooking is a natural part of our daily lives, but is this really the case? Cooking food gave us humans larger brains. In turn, we could develop new technologies, such as agriculture. 'How wonderful to walk through fields and meadows!' many people may cheerfully exclaim. They enjoy the 'natural environment.' But fields where only one crop grows – a monoculture – are far from natural: agriculture caused this. And though many people perceive agriculture as natural, it is a human-made technology. We humans adapted the crops. We humans use fire to cook our food. We changed our food, and, in turn, our food changed us. For example, the way we grow and eat food made our intestines shorter.

Agriculture: the first manifestation of Food Design.

According to Koert, we can therefore see agriculture as our first form of Food Design. 'A lot has changed concerning our understanding of what is and isn't natural. You can therefore imagine that in the future, we shall consider certain things to be natural that we do not yet consider to be so. I call this development Next Nature. Man is, by nature, a technological being. We always use tools and mould the world to suit us. What I find interesting about Next Nature is that we humans not only influence the world around us, but that it also influences us.'

Everything that grows autonomously – even if it is human-made – is natural.
Koert argues that, in this day and age, this proposition may be true. Though humans may have created traffic jams, computer viruses, digital networks, artificial intelligence and the financial system, these phenomena grow autonomously. Perhaps computer viruses are more natural today than, say, bananas. Bananas cannot reproduce without human intervention, yet computer viruses can spread unaided. It is ironic, to say the least, that many people think the banana is the erotic fruit par excellence due to its phallic shape. However, since it is seedless, it is the least fecund fruit imaginable. The banana we know today is nothing like the naturally occurring primordial banana, which is spherical and green and has spines and large seeds. Its flesh is nowhere near

as sweet as 'our' banana. Yet I don't know anyone who doesn't think a banana isn't natural. 'It grows in nature, doesn't it?!' The Cavendish banana is the most commonly eaten variety, and because it is cloned, it is genetically the same the world over. But this is hardly convenient, because any disease outbreak to which this banana is susceptible will wipe out all plantations in no time. Indeed, such a disease – fusarium fungi – already exists. In short, Next Nature is technology or its outcomes that we experience as natural. We have already embraced some technologies as natural, and it is interesting to think about the future with this in mind. Koert's Next Nature Network is a cultural organisation that makes ideas about our new, natural future so tangible that they already seem real. Only through life-like future scenarios can people truly imagine how new technology will be part of our lives. A glass of Nano Wine, for example, allows you to change its taste, from a Bordeaux to a Shiraz, in the microwave. Pharma Sushi is delicious sushi that also contains your required medication. Just because science is already working on these technologies, it doesn't mean people will understand how they impact their lives. 'By making it "real", I offer people the opportunity to envisage it. You can then investigate possible unintended side effects. For example, can someone with a large appetite overdose on sushi?'

Many factory-farmed animals cannot exist without human intervention.

The Next Nature Network's speculative works do not aim to predict the future. Koert makes possible futures, dreams and nightmares tangible so that people can already ask questions about such scenarios. A terrible idea helps when considering whether there are other options. And why is the idea – such as male pregnancy or working with robots – terrible? Is it because it seems 'unnatural'? This is precisely what Koert wants to show you: that 'natural' is an increasingly unclear concept. Perhaps this is what you have in mind when you think about coming times – an advanced digital future full of robotics. But we have been living with and in Next Nature for many years. Like the banana, many factory-farmed animals cannot exist without human intervention. A factory-farmed broiler chicken is born a living being. You could consider them natural, but these chickens have been bred to perfection and genetically engineered so that their parents remain fertile (otherwise, we would not have broiler chickens), but the broiler hardly 'wastes' any energy on developing reproductive organs.

Infertile fruit and animals grow faster and bigger.

Now you might think, 'I'm a vegetarian, and I don't like bananas, so what I eat is completely natural.' However, as you have just read, our agriculture is not natural. Carrots were not originally orange but yellow, white or purple. Because an orange carrot contains more beta carotene, it is visually appealing and sweeter than the 'natural' carrot. The orange carrot is now the standard worldwide.

You see more and more fruit without seeds.
The seeds of mandarins and grapes have been cultivated out of them because people don't want to be spitting out pips all the time. Apples and pears also have increasingly fewer seeds. Since there are fewer insects pollinating fruit trees, fruit framers opt for self-pollinating fruit varieties, allowing them to produce fruit without pollination. Some apple and pear varieties can do this due to a mutation that has changed their hormone balance. The Conference pear, for example, has very few seeds. Seedless watermelons have a longer shelf life and are 'triploid', which means they have three copies of each chromosome instead of two. Such plants' pollen and embryo sacs do not function properly, but they still produce fruit. Most bell peppers grown on a large scale are also sterile. Such cultivation is not only typical of fruit and vegetables. Some oysters are genetically modified. Since they do not spawn or reproduce, they can put all their energy into growing larger, and they can be harvested all year round.

Meat without death

In 1931, Sir Winston Churchill wrote that in the future, we should be rid of the absurd idea that we have to raise a chicken just to eat its fillet or wing. He predicted we would grow these parts separately. More than eighty years later, scientist Mark Post and food technologist Peter Verstrate presented the first hamburger made from cultured meat. The small disc was made from forty billion cultured cells grown in three months and cost 250,000 euros. 'What a hassle. Simply leave the meat out,' you may think – which is logical. But at present, people don't. The development of cultured meat has raised questions for Koert. 'Now that we can make meat in a lab, should we mindlessly make hamburgers en masse? It's an enormous development that upends our idea of what is natural – that you have to kill an animal for meat. Isn't this the ideal moment to rethink our food culture?'

Cultured meat is meat: a multiplication of animal stem cells. But its ramifications are different to what we now recognise as meat. The main difference is cultured meat does not require slaughtering animals. Hence, there is no need to farm masses of livestock. The suffering from intensive animal husbandry can stop, and factory farms – with their emissions – become a thing of the past. The growth, production and transport of animal feed are reduced so that much less water and raw materials are needed. The rainforest, frequently cut down to grow animal feed, can recover significantly, thus decreasing the nitrogen problem. Antibiotic resistance, resulting from the overuse of antibiotics in factory farming, is reduced. Viruses such as COVID, SARS, bird flu and swine fever are less likely to spread. As well as reducing the adverse effects of typical live-stock farming, there are also some interesting side effects. This new meat grows in a controlled environment, so it is not subject to infections, such as salmonella and E. coli, and means you can eat it raw. Diseases such as BSE (mad cow disease) will no longer occur, making bone mar-row more appealing to eat. In principle, you can grow any animal's cells. The flesh grows in long strands and can take the shape of a hamburger or even a banana.

How about a meatball made from Beyoncé's buttocks?

Koert, his team and a group of students investigated the implications of all this. What else is possible besides producing burgers? While beef and chicken are currently the main types of cultured meat, growing a piece of dolphin, puma or snake is also achievable. You could even breathe life into cellular material from extinct animals for a dodo fillet or dino steak with piri-piri sauce. And yes, we can also grow human flesh. How about a meatball made from Beyoncé's but-tocks, pâté made from Einstein's brain, or Lady Gaga in a dress made of her own flesh? Koert and his team published the cultured meat dishes they devised in The In Vitro Meat Cookbook, with forty-five recipes that you cannot cook yet. But who knows, maybe you'll be able to order them at 'Bistro in Vitro' in 2030. You can already view this virtual restaurant's menu, and they are taking bookings for the year 2030. Will you choose the meat gobstoppers followed by a meat-fruit dessert? You can also taste Pookie, which I think is one of the most beautiful Next Nature projects. Imagine: Pookie is your 'house pig'. He has lived in the backyard since he was a piglet. You cuddle him, your children play with him, and he eats all your daily leftovers. But he also goes to school every day in the form of a slice of sausage on a sandwich. You eat Pookie sausage; meanwhile, Pookie happily lives on in your backyard.

How does this thought affect your idea of meat?
Since real meat comes from a dead animal, is cultured meat cheating? What if this technology proves feasible and safe? Will it gradually change our understanding of what is 'natural'? Will cultured meat become the popular choice? Can this 'unnatural technology' also protect the climate and natural world and thus become nature? It is not Koert's goal to promote cultured meat. Instead, he wants to challenge people to take a broader view of this development, mainly because we are verging on a possible radical change in our understanding of meat. The debate about cultured meat initially focused on 'Frankenstein meat' and its feasibility and safety. The philosophical question 'what could it mean for us?' was hardly asked. The food at Bistro in Vitro is still in development, but in the meantime, the world's first cultured meat restaurant opened in Singapore in December 2020. The tasting menu costs twenty-three euros and contains three different dishes with cultured chicken meat. Singapore is the first country to allow the sale and consumption of cultured meat.

challenge

help build the Cavendish archive

Everyone is familiar with the supermarket and the kinds of fruit you find there. They often look uniform, with roughly the same shape, size, colours and standardised flavours. That's because many 'supermarket fruits' have been cloned or fertilised without pollinators.

The Cavendish banana is an extreme example of a cloned fruit. After tomatoes, bananas are the most eaten fruit globally – or number one if you regard tomatoes as a vegetable. The banana is the fourth largest crop grown worldwide. Incidentally, until the 1950s, you could find another cloned banana in the shops: the Gros Michel banana, which, according to insiders, tasted much better. You can now only taste it as the artificial banana flavour in processed food and sweets. Though this flavour is based on the Gros Michel banana and not the Cavendish, the former no longer exists because Panama disease wiped it out. Something similar could also happen to the Cavendish.

This small challenge, creating a collective Cavendish archive, is inspired by the effect of cloning. Because nowadays everyone has a 'cloning device' with the telephone in their pocket, let's make an archive of images of the banana. It's an ode to the Cavendish before it falls prey to fusarium fungi, and we've lost it for good. It's a doomsday scenario. After all, what's our smoothie, fruity dick pic or banana bread without our yellow friend?

the assignment

Do you see someone eating a banana? Take a picture of them!
Post it on instagram with the hashtag **#Cavendisharchive**

By the way... Bananas are slightly radioactive due to their high concentration of potassium, a mineral that is healthy for you. The banana's radioactivity is only a problem when eating hundreds of kilos of them. So I think their radioactivity is the least of your worries!

backwards

'I still remember it well. I was seventeen, and we were all offered therapy sessions through a large-scale government programme. Thanks to the new modifications to our digestive system, we could now eat rotten food without getting sick, but people couldn't get over their disgust. Hence the therapy sessions. I looked at my first plate of mouldy pasta and couldn't imagine taking a bite without gagging. I cautiously lifted the spoon and pulled off all the strands of slime. The food on my spoon looked like a spider spinning threads from each of its legs. It did not smell bad. That had already been taken care of because our perception of smell and taste had also been modified.'

Marion recounts, 'I had a hard time getting over the idea of eating rotten food. It was so repulsive. It was weird, though, because fermented food was trendy then. People were eating sauerkraut and kimchi and all kinds of blue cheeses. In Asia, they were way ahead. They had "hairy tofu" and nattō, those sticky fermented soybeans with stringy gunk. I gained many insights into how the human brain works. We learn to eat.'

'My mother had difficulty with it. Until she died, she was secretly binning a lot of old food. The fines didn't seem to bother her. In effect, we all had to go on re-education courses. That first bite of slimy pasta was actually pretty good to eat, but it still took me years to get properly used to it. I'm now fifty-two years old, and I always eat rotten food. If I'm honest, I sometimes let my food rot on purpose, because I've come to love the squishy layers of goo. It's an acquired taste. At the time, it was a daring move to combat food waste. But it was necessary. By 2022, a third of all food produced was wasted! Yes, the modification measures were essential

'The entire population received a microbial hyena adaptation using synthetic biology. People used to get sick from spoiled food, but hyenas can digest it. Advances in synthetic biology allowed us to digest rotten food too. Of course, there were riots and the whole anti-vaxxer movement. Some people thought they could eat spoiled food and not get sick – they got food poisoning. It was a turbulent time, but in the end, everyone went along with it. Wait, I'll get Paul. He works in the industry. A lot has changed for him and his colleagues since then.'

'We used to waste a lot of energy cooling food.'

Paul shares his recollections. 'You have to remember how much energy we used to waste cooling food! Everyone had refrigerators at home. If you went into a supermarket, there would be a low droning sound from the refrigerators and freezers. Every company in the industry had at least one refrigerated warehouse, and there were traffic jams full of refrigerated trucks. It's hard to imagine now, but this infrastructure of refrigerators on wheels crisscrossed the world. What a waste! We still have freezers for ice cream, but the enormous energy savings from scaling down the number of refrigerators has generated huge revenues. Huge revenues and an increase in the attainment of climate objectives.

'All it took was eliminating the expiry date. However, the one problem we had in the early years with all those uncooled food warehouses was the swarms of flies. It drove me crazy! So we developed a system for extracting the flies and feeding them to chickens. This is how we add value to a residual flow.'

backcasting

Imagine, in the future, synthetic biology will find a way of modifying our digestive system so that we can eat rotten food, just like hyenas do. Our smell and taste experience will also be modified, and nothing will stand in the way of us taking a dusty bite of a mouldy green sandwich. This absurd scenario, called the Human Hyena, was dreamt up by designer Paul Gong. He researched the possibility of adapting our bodies and proposes that inhaling genetically modified hyena bacteria will allow people to eat rotten food without getting sick. His well-worked-out project is a cynical reflection on our spiralling levels of food waste: a third of all food currently produced ends up as waste.

You can't predict or imagine the future, especially if you are looking through your contemporary glasses.

What would happen if you could digest rotten food? I am not talking about fermented food, because that is, of course, also rotten – but very healthy. This scenario of modifying our digestive system is hard to imagine given our current circumstances. But if you look back at the past, you will see that many things have happened that we once thought would never be possible. For example, we never thought we would have mass air transit and be boarding planes in the numbers we currently do. We never thought we would invent a material in which we could pack almost anything – moreover, a material that nearly all of us now have in our bodies: plastic. People didn't expect IVF to become a way to get pregnant. Or that COVID testing would become a routine occurrence. You cannot predict the future, especially if you only look at the future through your contemporary glasses, because everything in the present seems very normal. It is tempting to project current technological developments onto the future. Are drones, big data and blockchain the latest developments? If so, will the future have even more drones, bigger data, and blockchains that are even more secure? Perhaps. However, other possibilities are also conceivable. There could be something that sounds so illogical now that we can't even imagine it. Such as using mycelium to communicate telepathically with one another. Yet this is something scientists are currently researching.

Our future is ahead of us, right?
If you are asked to point to the future physically, chances are you will point ahead. And the past will be behind you. The Greeks and the Aymara, a people from the Andes mountains, see it exactly the other way around. They see the past as something ahead of them, and the future is behind them. You can see your past, and the future is unknown. You stand in a river and see the water flowing toward you. It flows along your legs, passes between them, and flows behind you, out of sight.

What if you take a huge step backwards into the future and look from there to the present? You don't have to define the time or place, but because you create this distance, you can speculate about it. You take a few decades step and look at the present through those contemporary glasses. You could be a grandparent reminiscing about your past and returning to where it all started. What I am describing here is what happens in speculative design. You envision a future that may seem utterly unrelated to the present and connect it with all kinds of fine threads. You connect your future scenario to a social effect, an environmental impact or a consequence of family relations. This allows you to build a web of threads that stretch from 'then' to 'now'. The web invites people to see a possible future. Maybe it's a terrible future. Perhaps you'll look forward to it. The more threads you connect to different aspects of human life, the more realistic the scenario seems and the more striking or unexpected side effects you discover. Maybe in the future, we will stop eating meat altogether, but we will also have a shortage of car tyres, bullets and paint because all those products depend on materials derived from pigs. Designer Christien Meindertsma made a book called Pig 05049 in which she inventories all of the different products to which a single pig contributed. Will there be halal sandpaper in the future?

Looking back from the future to the present as the past is called backcasting. By imagining that you are already in the future and describing the present as the past, you create space for looking at today's reality from a distance. It allows you to question the things that you currently consider normal. It's like being a fish that doesn't know it lives in water until someone holds it by its tail above the water and it sees the aquarium.

I have made exhibitions about the future of food. I made 'The Embassy of Food – Looking Back to Now' for Dutch Design Week. And I made a travelling exhibition in Canada called 'Edible Futures'. In the exhibition space were several speculative designs with possible future scenarios about food. There was Hanan Alkouh's butcher shop with meat cuts made from dulce seaweed and Chloé Rutzerveld's cabinet for designing and growing your own vegetables. Arvid & Marie made an autonomous robot called SAM that produces fermented beverages and presents itself as a legally defined business owner, and Hannerie Visser designed a pantry of products made from crops grown on saline water for when freshwater becomes scarce. And there were many more exciting ideas about food in the future.

You are not in the present.
You are in the past of the future.

It's easier to open yourself up to future scenarios if you travel through time first. With this in mind, the exhibition visitors had pre-recorded stories to listen to about how each design had become a reality in the future. To prevent food waste, consuming rotten food, like a hyena, became a reasonable proposition. The absence of fresh water for growing crops already seemed like a reality. You heard a voice proclaiming in amazement that the West used clean drinking water for flushing toilets. What decadence! 'Nowadays, it is difficult to grow green beans because they cannot tolerate salt. You can still buy them, but they are much more expensive because they are grown with desalinated water. Therefore we now make fake beans, from wheat and barley, that grow better on saline soil.'

As you wandered around the exhibition, you were transported to that future and realised that it all might happen one day. Mouldy sandwiches in your lunch box. How absurd! Or is it? By reflecting on our present-day reality from a future perspective, you could see a different absurdity: a time when we wasted half of the bread we produced. Doubt begins to set in. You are not in the present. You are in the past of the future. By making different choices now, you can start writing a new story.

challenge

top 3 future absurdities

Imagine you are in the last phase of your life. (Perhaps you already are.) You can probably apply the principle of Backcasting rather well. A colleague once told me that he found it much more fun to do creative workshops with the elderly because they are not surprised by change. Young people often think that the current world is the only option. So imagine that you are at the end of your life and look back to the present.

Look around you with a view from the future and explore your food environment. Look at how antiquated it all is! Can you see things that we consider normal now but may find absurd in the future? Can you be a fish that observes the water it is in?

Make a top three of food things you think will disappear or change in the future and make a photo or video of each of them. Post them on instagram and add your memory of them, written by the future 'old' you. Maybe tell what life is like in the future now that this thing has changed or gone. Use #backcasting and tag @lickit.book

If you use a calendar app, make an appointment with yourself for ten years in the future and write about the above phenomena. Has any progress been made by then? (Hopefully, you'll still be using the same app. Or maybe our calendars will have changed completely?)

Top 3 things we consider normal now that you think will disappear or change in the future:

1.

2.

3.

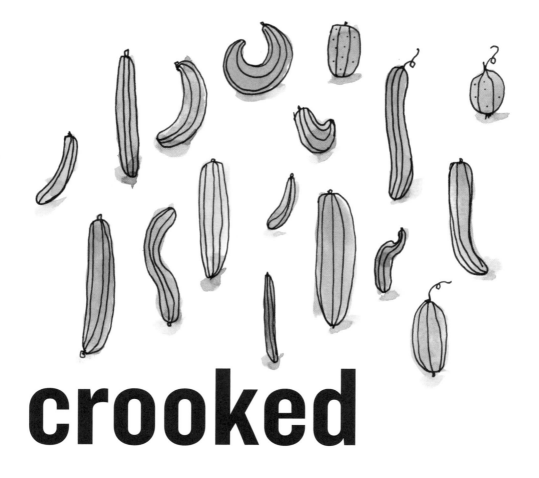

crooked

Now that I am forty-four years old, my life looks like this: I have three children, two daughters and a son. My oldest has a different father than the youngest two. I am not with either father, and I co-parent with them both. When the children are not with me, I work a lot, and when they are, I do little work so I can spend a lot of time with them. I have a cat and a dog. Though I do not live with my boyfriend, we share taking care of the dog. Do I see you raising an eyebrow?

I can understand if you are. Maybe you have a different idea of what families ought to be like. Nevertheless, I'm very happy, and our bond as a family is very strong. My life has allowed me to learn, grow, and become the best and most loving version of myself. My life constellation raises eyebrows, usually from people who don't know me. My chosen life deviates from the norm, giving many people a vague, awkward feeling. As if something isn't right. When my household travels together, we have four different surnames as a family. This can be confusing. On the other hand, the first names of the children and the dog are connected. Their names are Juni, Januari (Dutch for June and January) and April, and the dog is called Winter. But these names are not that common in the Netherlands. So, in this sense, we are outside the norm.

What is a norm?

Norms are unwritten rules about how you should behave. Or, in this case, about how you should lead your life. Norms help people to know what 'normal' is. Normal simply means within the norm, and our minds use it as a benchmark. From a practical point of view, it helps to know it's the norm to pay in advance when you have food delivered and afterwards when you eat in a restaurant. Knowing this means you don't always have to ask: 'Do I pay in advance? Do I pay per course? Is it on account, or can I wash dishes with my sexy body?' It is also the norm that you don't haggle at the supermarket, and you don't cook for yourself at a restaurant. Though this is all very logical, I don't see it as a written rule anywhere. Norms are helpful for our brains, so we don't have to keep wondering what is or isn't socially acceptable in certain situations. The world is complicated enough already. Now we can concentrate on other things. For example, think about how strange would it be if you pulled out your hand blender in a luxury restaurant to blitz the food. The offended red-faced chef would throw you out – but not before you ask for a doggy bag – after which you would go straight to your sick mother, who can't chew, and feed her the food.

Norms are often mentioned together with values.

They belong together like tomatoes and Italy. And that's rather strange because tomatoes originally came from South America and were not red but yellow. Hence 'pomo d'oro', meaning 'golden apple'. It's the same with norms and values. They seem inextricably linked, but values can exist without norms, whereas the reverse isn't necessarily the case. Tomatoes can exist without Italy, but imagine Italy without tomatoes! Though the Italians would survive, they would probably be hugely depressed and eat their tomato-less pasta crying every night.

Norms are the unspoken rules concerning how you should behave. Values are the underlying ideals that shape the norm. A value could be: 'I think it's important to spend time with the family.' A norm that might follow from this could be: 'We eat together at the table.' (And, therefore, not alone and naked in bed, chewing to the rhythm of 'Another One Bites the Dust'.) Norms are crazy things because they are invisible. The presence of norms is so logical that you often don't even realise they are there. And yet they largely determine how you behave and what you think. If spending time with the family is a value from which eating together at the table becomes a norm, wouldn't eating together in bed also be a good norm? Sometimes breaking the norm brings you closer to your values.

In Europe, you preferably make as little noise as possible when eating. In China, slurping and belching are quite normal.

Your culture, rather than you personally, often determines your norms. In Europe, you make as little noise as possible when eating and don't talk with your mouth full. In China, talking with your mouth full, slurping and belching are quite normal. A culture passes on its norms, but the media also moulds and expands them. Although commercials of men preparing large cuts of meat are much less common nowadays, the carnivorous, barbecuing, beer-drinking, buttock-scratching man is still entrenched in our collective perception of men – and meat. That man, who probably also frequently belches, is married to another stereotype: the cleaning, caring and cooking woman, who is also sexy – but not overly, just a little. In exchange for her caring, he earns the money. She also works (hey, she's an emancipated woman!), but he earns more, so besides her job, she also takes care of the food, the household and the children. He also cooks. Usually when he puts on his 'kiss the cook' apron on summer Sundays and makes his speciality: barbecue chicken with a can of beer up its ass. We can all picture this and mostly find it funny because reality isn't so stereotypical. You probably know many more people who do not resemble the description above. Yet women are still paid less than men to do the same work. And they still take on most of the unpaid care work. Most chefs are male: they also cook but are paid for their work.

When it comes to food, we have to deal with countless norms.
Every culture's food comes with extensive etiquette. (As an aside, the word 'enormous' originally meant 'exception to the norm'.) Parents desperately try to force their children to eat with a knife and fork 'because you never know when you'll be invited to the Queen's for dinner.' Eating rules that conform to religion, identity (following a trend diet, for example) or gender also influence our behaviour. Men are therefore less likely to buy the curvaceously 'feminine' macaroon. However, this might be different if the macaroon is square and has a less pretty colour. Men also like sweet foods. We should also consider the person who prepares food when thinking about norms. Traditionally, women worked in kitchens, but then more women started ascending the career ladder. Thus women with a migratory background who were usually poorly paid began making food in factories, canteens and restaurants. The stereotypes I describe above are heteronormative. This is the predominant 'universal' standard from which we subconsciously consider whether something falls within the norm and is, therefore, normal. As well as norms based on sexuality, you also have norms based on skin colour, body shape, accent, clothing, and so on.'

Norms are invisible, so you often only realise something as normative when you fall outside of it. Suppose the woman in a heteronormative family always changes the diapers. The man will not notice that the changing mat at restaurants is often in the women's toilet. This fact only becomes noticeable when the man, with a screaming, smelly baby, nervously asks at the bar for the changing facilities. Similarly, the popularity of family discounts and 'tables for four' becomes an issue when you dine alone in restaurants. If you conform to the norm, your behaviour will be appropriate to each situation. However, there are more ways to behave outside the norm than within it. You can order a burger at a drive-thru in many more ways than everyone else does. You can do it dancing, singing or with a presentation of drawings. You won't hurt anyone, but it will still arouse disapproval from some. Many people simply find it uncomfortable to step outside the norm. The norm gives them clarity and guidance. Once outside the norm, people must constantly consider whether their behaviour fits their values. This costs the brain significant energy, so it is easier to reject such ideas.

Questioning the norm is the domain of 'queering'. 'Queer' comes from the Irish word 'curare' and denotes something crooked or bent. It stands for the 'unusual' or 'strange'. Robert Adolfsson teaches Queering Practices at Design Academy Eindhoven and tells me about when homosexuality was still forbidden and even a criminal act. 'The homosexual was clearly outside the norm at the time and was denounced as "queer". Everything that fell outside the norm at the time was considered strange. Queering Practices is, therefore, about alienation and questioning the norm. Within the design education context, it is interesting to consider that many designs have traditionally been just as heteronormative. Therefore, design also excludes people. We ask how you can design more inclusively as a designer by making invisible norms visible.' Hence 'queering' is a verb, a way of looking and questioning. Some say the word also comes from 'questioning', which is precisely what it does. It doesn't have to be about sexual orientation, though that is from where the expression derives. What was an insult has now become a catch-all term for those who feel different and want to operate outside the norm. 'It indicates the will to move beyond the norm and celebrates that area as a new territory that is brash, exuberant and without judgment or set rules,' says Robert.

Falling outside the norm can be liberating and does not mean giving up your values.

Queering mainly questions dominant and oppressive norms, but I think it is interesting to question all norms. In his book The Queer Art of Failure, Jack Halberstam argues that revolution lies in the everyday. Falling outside the norm can also be liberating: you don't have to prove yourself, and you gain considerable freedom in return. Moreover, venturing outside of norms does not mean giving up your values. And that's what makes it so interesting! Which norms do you live by? Perhaps setting new norms will strengthen your personal values. If spending time together as a family is one of your values, then eating in bed together may be much more valuable than mindlessly munching on food together at the table every day.

Norms are not necessarily bad. It depends on the motivations behind them. When they unconsciously control you, it is time to take out your queering glasses, dust them off, and put them on. It's time to explore your norms. Without judgment or prejudice, take a look at how you eat, how you live, and why you do the things you do. (See also chapter Afrocado.) Why is something the norm? Who determines this? What do you think could be 'queer food', in the sense of the verb? What – what act – would make the food queer? I asked this question on Instagram and got a flood of tantalising answers, such as:

- **Food with faces on it**. Especially food that's usually presented as naturally as possible. A salad with eggs for the eyes and a slice of avocado for the mouth. Salad should always look 'tasty', 'natural' or 'sexy'. With a face, it becomes crazy, childish and non-traditional.
- **White food.** In physics, colour is visible as light with a specific frequency. Black and white are not colours, because they have no specific frequency, but white light has the frequencies of all colours within it.
- **Pizza with pineapple.** This pizza hasn't had it easy, and some people still will not tolerate it.
- **Artificial flavours.** They are not natural flavours but attempt to taste like something from a natural source. If you eat something with chemically developed flavours, you are eating something 'phoney'.
- **Tomatoes.** Grown as a fruit, eaten as a vegetable, drunk as juice, cooked into jam, and ultimately, what does it matter? They're delicious, and we all enjoy them.
- **Nocturnal binge eating.** It's a sneaky activity because it's often unseen and almost a form of rebellion, like eating dinner for breakfast. And who says you can't eat cornflakes for dinner?

you Cannot — unsee me

Queer exists by virtue of the norm.

If you want to define queer food, you end up in a grey area. It is not without reason that the essence of queer is indefinable. The norm is defined. Everything beyond is queer, which makes it difficult to explain. Queer exists by virtue of the norm, but norms also shift. So what was queer may later become the norm. Queering as a way of thinking is much more interesting than 'queer' labels. Robert envisages a restaurant placed directly next to a waste container of a normative restaurant. 'YES!' he shouts. 'That sounds great! They sell the food that is discarded due to social norms even though it is still edible. No, it won't be repurposed. Nothing new is cooked from it. It is just being sold as it is. Raw and uninhibited. That would be queer food for me.'

Queering as a way of thinking is much more interesting than 'queer' labels.

The surroundings and context make food queer, says Robert. 'One minute it's a delicious dish, the next it's garbage. Why is it now disgusting if you take it out of the dumpster undamaged and nothing has happened to it? Why is it distasteful? What makes it unpalatable? That's what makes it so interesting to me. The situation creates a sense of alienation and places food outside the norm. However, the food still tastes the same. That's why I wouldn't want it to be served differently. Why would a restyle make it good again?'

challenge

chew and knead your meat chewing gum

Have you ever chewed gum without a mouth? Maybe with your ears or nose? Or with your hands? Normally, you wouldn't think about these kinds of possibilities, but nothing is normal when it comes to chewing gum. It is flexible and constantly adapts. It fits under the table, on the wall and in the waste bin. It sticks in your hair, falls apart with peanut butter, and turns white if you chew it for too long. Compared to chewing gum, you are a hard, inflexible stone.

This challenge takes you through the chewing gum making process. By making it yourself, you will discover how chewing gum can become something else. This chewing gum has endless possibilities. Can you be as flexible as this chewing gum?

ingrediënten (1 serving):
- **25 g** (6 tsp) of **white wheat flour** without added yeast or baking powder
- **12 ml** (3 tsp) of bottled **beet juice** (or other juice with no chunks or pulp)

here's how you do it!

Making basic chewing gum*
- Mix the flour and beet juice. If the flour still seems a bit dry, add a bit more fluid, being careful not to add too much.
- Knead the dough on a clean surface for about 10 minutes.
  You will feel it change from sticky to soft and elastic.
- Wrap the dough in cling film and place it in a plastic container.
  Let it rest for 30 minutes at room temperature.
- Take a bowl containing about 2 to 3 centimetres of water.
  It should be enough to submerge the dough in water.
- You are now going to 'wash' the dough and knead it under the water by pulling it out and pushing it together. After a while, you will see a white liquid seeping out of the dough: this is the starch. Wash out as much starch as possible. What's left is gluten. This is the flour protein.
- After about 5 minutes of washing, the dough is elastic like chewing gum.
  Chew it in your mouth to feel the effect.

* Unfortunately, this recipe is not for you if you have a gluten allergy.

tips:
- For best results, use flour containing 12% or more protein content.
- Try different types of juice for other colours.
- The ratio of flour to liquid is 2:1.

turn your hard work into something special!

Baking chewing gum
- Add your favourite savoury condiment (soy sauce, chilli or salt and pepper) to your gum.
- Put a frying pan over medium heat and add a drop of oil.
- When the oil is hot, place the chewing gum in the pan.
- Flatten the gum with a spatula so that it cooks evenly. Fry until golden brown.
- Remove your chewing gum from the pan and let it cool.

Enjoy your meal!

Yes, it seems gross, but this recipe is based on seitan: a natural meat substitute made from wheat gluten. So it is mainly your head and norms that can stretch a little more.

what
a
challenge
huh?

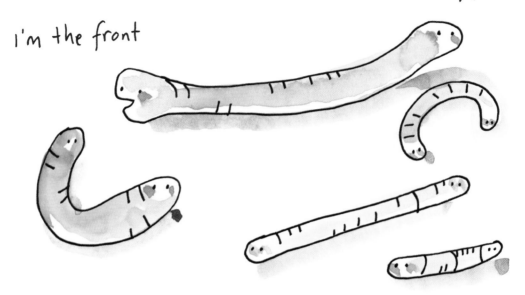

i'm the front

no, I am!

afrocado

One morning my oldest daughter, then just three years old, looked at her father as he put the Christmas baubles away in a box. 'What are you going to do with them?' she asked, her eyes following his hands. 'They're going into the attic until next year,' he replied. Her mouth dropped open in delighted wonder. 'Will there be a Christmas next year too?'

What is the meaning of life?
Ha ha! You probably didn't expect that in a book about food, did you?
Here's how philosopher Alan Watts describes life's meaning. 'The meaning of life is just to be alive. It is so plain and so obvious and so simple. And yet, everybody rushes around in a great panic as if it were necessary to achieve something beyond themselves.'

I don't claim to know the meaning of life. Thinking about it, though, can give you some good food ideas. When we think and talk about food, we often refer to it as a fundamental human necessity for survival. And that survival is the meaning of life. We tend to avoid death. All life must eat, yet all life eventually dies. So what is the point?

Is there a purpose? Not really. In fact, it doesn't matter at all.

Watts asks you to imagine an organism as a tube. A tube where something goes in on one end, and something comes out on the other. We developed some extra parts on one end of the tube, such as eyes, ears, a brain and taste buds. These extra parts allow us to better 'catch' the food to put it in the tube. The tube gradually deteriorates until it wears out and dies. We've managed to slow down the deterioration process slightly. Sometimes an offspring – a new little tube – comes out of the tube. That's how it goes. Is there a purpose? Is there a point we are all working toward? Is there an ultimate tube we aspire to be somewhere in the future? Not really. In fact, it doesn't matter at all.

You may think that Alan Watts's worldview is nihilistic, but that's certainly not true. Although the example of the tube ignores feelings, there are times when we feel deeply connected to life and to others, such as while walking in nature. The forest's beauty and complexity overwhelm you. So much so that you forget to think. You become absorbed in the moment, filled with a sense of connectedness. You exist, and that is all. The same thing can happen when you dance or listen to music. Your thoughts subside, and you feel life flowing through you. You are present in no other moment than the now. You don't think about how you danced yesterday or tomorrow's sore muscles. You don't think about others staring at or judging you. You have nothing to prove or hide. You are at one with everything around you.

Watts states: 'Does music have any point or purpose? Is your dancing meant to get you to the other side of the dance floor? Is the purpose of a piece of music to get to the final chord as quickly as possible? If so, the best musician would be whoever can make the shortest piece, with only closing chords. But, thankfully, this is not the case. You dance for the sake of dancing. You listen to music because you want to hear, feel and experience its sounds. You eat and taste because it gives you pleasure.' And because you want to stay alive. But if that were the only reason, then a diet of water, bread and supplements would suffice.

The point of life is it does not have a point.
The point of a circle is it does not have a point. And in pointlessness, we can find the real meaning of life. We call the things we do for pleasure and are not directly useful or productive 'playing'. The word 'play' comes from the Middle Dutch 'pleien', which means 'to keep oneself busy' or 'to take care of'. In turn, this comes from the English 'plight', which means 'promise' but also 'danger' and 'risk'. Is there promise and danger in playing? Are we perhaps made for play, as all mammal offspring universally do? Children socialise while playing and learn about risk. Adults often play by seeking risks, such as going to the casino, racing or kitesurfing. We do not treat playing adults seriously. So our children become an excuse for the secret enjoyment of playing with Lego. And so you get all your kicks from a one-week skiing holiday that you've earned through a

year of hard work. However, playing is also beneficial. People who play have a more flexible brain structure than those who hardly or never play. Moreover, those who play little in childhood are more likely to develop behavioural problems later.

If you ask me why I had children, my answer will have nothing to do with how useful it is. Children take up a lot of time, money and energy. Babies are not practical. They regularly puke on you with a surprised look on their face when you're just about to leave the house to make an important presentation in your crisply ironed dress. My answer would be about the intense sense of connection I experience with my children. They surprise me in the most ordinary moments. When, on a grey day, my youngest calls avocados 'afrocados' and talks about 'paused eggs' instead of poached eggs. Then I feel intensely happy. Does it make sense? No. Is it satisfying? Absolutely.

Children are the perfect alibi for eating under rather than at the table.

Why is the adult world so concerned with being useful when we all know that life's true value lies elsewhere? We derive the most happiness from the intangible, from things that do not serve a direct purpose. Even Nietzsche, known for being inhibited, said he would only believe in a God who knows how to dance. Without music, life would be a mistake. Nietzsche believed humans are innovative creators who should approach life with cheerful seriousness. This is easy for children but much more difficult for adults. With a child by your side, you can easily jump in or dance strangely around a fountain together. People will certainly think you're crazy if you do such things alone. Children are the perfect alibi for eating under rather than at the table. Or cut spaghetti with scissors, like Pippi Longstocking, or lick food off the table. Do you think you shouldn't play with your food? Though most parents tell their children this, they mean that you should respect your food. (And they probably don't want to clean up the mess.) Moreover, playing with food is impractical. If you wish to peel every grape at breakfast, you will probably be late for school.

It should be noted that children don't always look at food with an open mind. I once sprinkled basil leaves over the pasta. My son looked startled at the plate and then angrily inquired, 'Why are you putting leaves on it?' as if I had spoiled his pasta with some random leaves picked up from the ground. Some knowledge and experience can certainly help you along, but do they have to restrict a playful spirit?

Everyone was once a child. I think a small part of us will always remain a child. In fact, a childlike perspective underscores my elementary design principles. I try to look at and interrogate the world around me with a childlike eye. Why don't we eat under the dining table? Can I get strangers to feed each other without too much discomfort? Why do we mimic animal meat with meat substitutes?

Sometimes people ask whether my work is culturally determined and understood in all cultures. However, my work is concerned not with a country's culinary culture but with what lies beneath it. It's not about whether you put Parmesan on spaghetti vongole. (Don't!) It's about the eating human being. And it just so happens that people who eat also play. I gradually discovered that people have significant differences in food culture, but under that 'cultural fabric', we are actually very similar. We are curious and shy. We go to sleep, have sorrows and can laugh. We can be in love. And we want to be seen. And somewhere in all of us lurks a child. If you can reach the child inside the person, you don't need much cultural context. Besides, children love skipping outside the cultural rules.

Sometimes you need a child's perspective to appreciate how we deal with food. It can be strange and lead to new questions.
Why don't we eat in the shower?
Why do we throw away a carrot's green shoots when they are edible?
Why do we eat on the terrace at a restaurant but not picnic on the pavement next to it?

Like five-year-olds, we should ask 'why' a little more often. Not to find the answers but to discover whether we can do something differently. The answer to this question shouldn't be, 'Because I say so', but rather, 'Yes indeed, good question!' And thus, 'Why not!

The guests sat under huge purpose-built tables at a travelling dinner I once made in India. I covered the tables with large white tablecloths. From the outside, you saw massive white tables. But when the fairy lights under the tables illuminated, you could see the space underneath through the luminescent white fabric. Fragrant flower garlands and etagères laden with delicious snacks hung from the underside of the tables. The guests – adults – sat beneath on chairs without legs. Comfort, service and delicious food are essential to make the difference between an interesting and an infantile experience: something playful, not childish. As I walked around, ducking under the tablecloth now and then, I saw faces gleaming with delight. These guests were from the affluent class and quite spoiled in terms of dining experiences.

Nevertheless, this dinner still challenged the guests and made them feel special. Some of them said it took them back to their childhood. The experience was both pleasant and disarming. The principle of the amazed gnome applies here. Imagine you're a gnome who suddenly finds itself in the human world. Everything you see is new, and you take nothing for granted. So what do you see?

Look around like an amazed gnome. It leads to new perspectives.

Jan Buiter was a professor of business sociology at Erasmus University Rotterdam. He came up with the idea of the 'amazed gnome' as a methodology for business organisations. It works as follows. When dealing with a particular issue, you shouldn't put science first. Instead, you should passionately strive to connect to the subject. You must want to prod it and make love to it a little. You will only find new entry points by being very curious and questioning everything.

Why copy dead animals when the protein structures give you a toolbox to create something new?

In the supermarket, I like to look around as if I'm an amazed gnome. As far as I'm concerned, this place beautifully encapsulates society. Something that caught my attention years ago is the rapidly growing shelf of meat substitutes. Next to the sausages, meatballs and burgers are surrogate sausages, meatballs and burgers made of vegetable matter. There's nothing wrong with this. It's helpful if you don't want to eat meat but want to eat something that resembles it. Besides, by choosing not to eat meat, you are contributing to a better world. What bothers me is the production of meat substitutes is based on the 'original' meat. Meat is the original, whereas the meat substitute is a copy, and copies are always inferior. You can copy a Van Gogh as much as you can mess around with it, yet it will always be a copy and therefore less valuable than the original. The same is true for meat substitutes. Vegetarians deserve a superior version precisely because they make a sustainable choice. Furthermore, 'original' meat often comes from animals that have suffered terribly. Why would you want to imitate this? The shapeless protein structures of meat substitutes have not been put through such misery.

What if we look at the question of substitute meat with a childlike eye and create fantasy animals? Animals with their own narrative, not associated with factory farming – vegetarian animals whose habitat, lifestyle and diet determine the final product. I designed four animals as a vegetarian alternative. The first is the 'ponti', an animal that lives in extinct volcanoes and has a large population in Hawaii. The ponti nibbles on volcano ash, which gives their meat a mildly smoked flavour. It builds its nests by using its rigid tail to make holes in the solidified magma. This stiff tail makes a delicious party snack that you chew the meat off and keep your hands clean. Another vegetarian animal is the 'herbast'. It lives in the southern French herb fields, where the crops make a perfect hiding place. It is prey for many predators, but its fur made of natural herbs gives it the ideal camouflage. The herbast is challenging to find, which makes it a bit more expensive. But if you can catch one, they are already pre-seasoned, and the pieces of herbaceous stir-fry meat are pan-ready. The herbast's rectangular shape makes it ideal for packaging and transport. Its shape is also perfect for preparing and slicing as a roast; everyone can have an equal portion. I also came up with a vegetarian fish called the 'biccio', with green stripes through its flesh. These indicate an increased antioxidant level due to the large amount of seaweed it eats off the coast of Japan.

A biccio fillet looks special, making this vegetarian fish very suitable for sushi or sashimi. Finally, there is a vegetarian bird called the 'sapicu'. It lives in the Canadian maple forests, where it eats the resin and sap of this tree, as maple syrup. This bird's meat is tender with a sweet-savoury flavour. It is the ideal dessert meat and pairs well with ice cream and chocolate. I consiously chose to design animals instead of abstract shapes. The animals you find in the supermarket are fantasy animals as well.

Ponti

delicately ↙ smoked meat

firm tail

herbal fur

Herbast

Biccio

filet

You can simultaneously be conscious of the fact that life leads nowhere and feel connected to it. The essential element in this proposition is play. You may be overwhelmed by thinking about the world's problems and how to solve them. Many of these problems stem from our eating habits, what we eat, and where we get our food. Are you worried you can't contribute to the 'greater good' in a playful way? I believe that you can. Stressed people, driven by deadlines, have no room in their heads to come up with other solutions. However, if you play and don't take life too seriously, you will be more creative, energetic and full of life. Who eats with more respect: someone who marvels at the flavours of a simple dish or someone who is stressed out and thoughtlessly gobbles down their food?

Playing is the key to more connectedness, freedom and appreciation.

Nobody has to give you the freedom to play. You already have that freedom. The more you play, the freer you feel. The freer you feel, the more space there is in your head for pleasure and gratitude. And with this growing sense of gratitude, you will appreciate your food more.

challenge

eat in the shower!

You might think that sitting is sitting. No one told you as a child that there is an essential difference between 1) sitting in the bath and 2) sitting on a chair at the dining table. You found out for yourself when you lost your ice cream in the pool, and no matter how hard you tried, you couldn't get it back intact. For this challenge, we are going back to your childhood but without the ice cream.

instructions

Take an orange with you into the shower. Peel it while you're in the shower and eat it. The warm running water causes the orange peel to release many essential oils and radiate a wonderful fragrance. Bite into the juicy flesh and feel the juice run down your body as it mixes with the water.

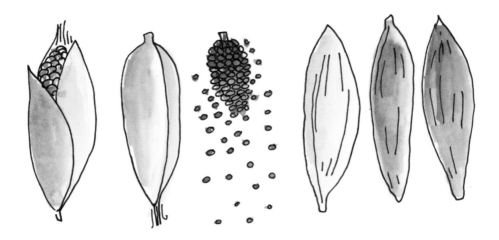

power

'If I win this award, I will buy a tractor.' I was a jury member for the Future Food Design Awards. This answer from one of the nominees surprised me. Designers usually want to use the prize money to make a better prototype or showcase their endeavour on a prestigious platform.

Mexican designer Fernando Laposse had other plans for the prize money. He had made a series of extraordinary objects – veneered vases and lamps in beautiful colours, from deep purple to pale yellow and pink. The veneer is derived from the husks of Mexican heirloom corn varieties, has a beautiful grain structure, and comes in unbelievable colours from purple-blue to candy pink. Unfortunately, these heirloom species are endangered. International trade agreements, aggressive use of pesticides, and large-scale cultivation of modern yellow production corn threaten biodiversity and erode the soil. Yellow corn is mainly produced as animal feed or to make bioplastics and sweeteners. This requires a standardised product that can only be achieved with genetically modified hybrid seeds. The old crops are lost, and the soil becomes exhausted. Many Mexican farmers cannot quickly return to growing their traditional multicoloured corn. They already live in poverty, and these traditional varieties are less profitable than the commercial ones. Only the indigenous population still cultivates these species.

Fernando works on this project with a small community of farmers and herders in Tonahuixtla, who still grow these corn varieties. Fernando's products use corn husks, the part that is typically thrown away. He has developed a simple technique for making veneers from the beautifully coloured leaves and applies this to products, from vases to folding screens. By reducing waste, he creates a higher yield for the farmers who now sell the corn and its husks. Fernando has taught a group of local women to make the veneer to generate their own income. The beautiful colours of the traditional corn give the veneer a unique and diverse colour palette.

Food is power, but creative thinking can shift that power.

The unique objects Fernando creates and sells in leading galleries allow him to invest in sowing more land with heirloom corn seeds. In collaboration with CIMMYT, 'the world's largest corn seed bank', he is helping the local community to go back to their traditional maize crops step by step. A tractor comes in handy for this. Fernando ended up winning both the jury prize and the audience prize. Hardly surprising, given that his work is a solid example of how design can be beautiful and bring about gradual change. Food is power, but creative thinking can shift that power.

Pittsburgh in Pennsylvania has many restaurants, from Chinese to Italian, Turkish and Belgian. Despite this variety, there are cuisines you cannot find in 'Steel City'. There are no Palestinian, North Korean or Haudenosaunee restaurants – at least, not permanently. If you walked around Pittsburgh between 2010 and 2017, you might have seen a small kiosk whose striking exterior was re-clad every three to five months with bold, colourful patterns and large graphic elements. Conflict Kitchen, an idea by Jon Rubin and Dawn Weleski, only served food from nations with which the US was in conflict. They would regularly change the menu, the placemats and the backgrounds and origin of the food. With each new version of the concept, the restaurant collaborated with local initiatives of the respective food source.

During its existence, the kiosk served food from Iran, Afghanistan, Cuba, North Korea, Venezuela and a confederacy of six First Nations peoples called Haudenosaunee. They presented the food with a specially made newspaper and a placemat, and even the packaging had a story. When I spoke to Jon at a conference long ago, he told me that food is one of the best information conveyors. Maybe you don't want to read about the food's background and just want to eat good fare. That's allowed too. Nevertheless, if you do eat and read something on the placement that arouses your interest, you may well immerse yourself in the situation and the people in 'that other country'. Jon says that many people in the US only receive polarised narratives about nations in conflict and often have no idea what it's like in those countries. Who lives there, what do they think and feel, and what do they eat? Through the media lens, North Korea appears to be nothing but a grey zone on the world map.

Food can change this polarised narrative because it is a potent information medium. If you invite people into a room to speak about the conflicts of the US, you probably only attract a small niche audience. If you serve good food and show how people live in that other, unknown and feared country, you have a bigger chance of arousing interest. Maybe not right away. Perhaps people initially come because they're hungry. But if the food tastes good, they might come back. And then perhaps there will be interest in the origin and background of those flavours. Jon explains that they could have implemented the project in many ways, but the choice for a commercial entity – a kiosk – was conscious. It allowed the project to partly support itself and align with something with which many Americans are already familiar. It probably would have reached only a small elite group as a standalone art project.

Besides cooking and serving food, Conflict Kitchen also organised events. These didn't always go well. In 2014, the restaurant was closed for four days. They received death threats after introducing a Palestinian menu. Conflict Kitchen received accusations of spreading one-sided information. Jon, who is Jewish, stated that, as with the other editions, the aim was to provide more insight; this time, it was about the Palestinian perspective.

Food has always been politically charged.
Even in the time of hunter-gatherers, there was a division of power. Who brought in meat? Who had the best skills for finding food, and how was it distributed? Did the strong support the weak? Were children protected and fed? Whoever wants to conquer a country ensures that the water and food supply is cut off. Our dependence on food makes it the perfect leverage. All other raw materials, such as oil and gas, are primarily needed to produce food. We are driven by the will to live, and to live requires food. Food underlies everything we do. As long as we live together, we are dealing with the distribution of power.

Politics is often invisible, but its effects affect us every day.

I was once in a car with Michael Pollan driving to a restaurant near Camden, Maine. He had just given a compelling talk – a performance of his now well-known act. He walked on stage carrying a McDonald's bag, took out a quarter pounder with cheese and held it in the air as he asked the audience, 'How much oil are we eating?' He poured thick black oil into four glasses. That's how much oil it takes to make one burger. Not for cooking; this is about petroleum. 'Eating is an agricultural act' is a famous quote by the farmer and activist Wendell Berry. Whoever eats is doing agriculture and thus also shapes the world. As we look at the landscape from the car, I ask Michael about his interest in food. He is currently working on a study into psychoactive substances, or drugs. Michael elaborates: 'No, that's not food. Or maybe it is. You put them in your body. Laws have been constructed around them. Perhaps psychoactive substances are the most restricted food. Ha ha! We often only talk about these laws, but I'd like to know what is behind them. These laws mean our opinions on these substances are one-sided. I want to know what else there is to discover. I'm not an expert, just a curious amateur. And it is precisely because I am not an expert – not a cook, dietician or producer – that I can discover connections others don't see.' Politics is invisible, particularly in our food, but its effects affect us daily and more than we think. As the car pulls into the yard, Michael concludes, referring to Wendell Berry, 'Eating is a political act.'

What do you think of when you hear the word 'food'? Depending on their cultural background, people will give different answers. Yet flavour and socialising are the top answers. Most people have a very romantic and positive association with food. Other answers are diet, sustainability, health and sometimes frustration. I hardly ever hear politics given as an answer, even though food and politics are inextricably linked – perhaps that innocent elderberry on the bush may not think so. And neither do you when you pick the berry and put it in your mouth. Why is food political? And why don't we see it as such?

Do you like thick American pizza with extra cheese?
One where the melted cheese threads spill from all sides, searching for redemption. One where your teeth sink gum-deep into a warm, chewy mass of salty goo. For some, it's a gastronomic reverie; for others, a nightmare. Whichever camp you're in, thick cheese pizza sales have rocketed in recent years. In 2009, Domino's started topping their pizzas with forty per cent more cheese. Before then, things weren't looking good for Domino's, which was dealing with a double whammy of alarming financial figures and a bad image. Fortunately for them, an organisation called Dairy Management helped Domino's develop new pizzas with forty per cent more cheese. In addition, the company pumped twelve million dollars into an extensive marketing campaign. It worked! Consumers overwhelmingly fell for the fatty cheese slices, and the money poured in. Dairy Management is an American government organisation. Why does the government want Americans to eat more cheese? It is a response to another government programme urging Americans to eat less saturated fat. The consumption of skimmed milk products increased as a result, as did the surplus of whole milk. They must have asked themselves: 'What are we supposed to do with all that milk fat?' Consequently, some of it went to the cheese pizzas. What was taken out of one side was put back in the other. Americans now eat three times as much cheese as they did in the 1970s.

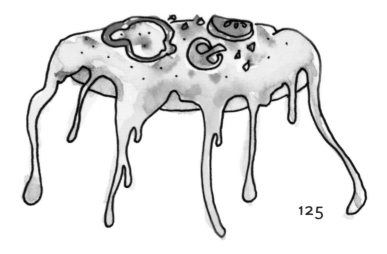

125

Politics and food belong together like water and bread. Although you, as an innocent consumer of gross fatty pizzas, probably won't notice. When the war broke out in Ukraine, social media turned yellow and blue shortly after. Fabio Parasecoli posted a photo from Poland on his instagram account. A casual image of a market stall selling pierogi, small dough dumplings filled with potato and cheese. There was an accompanying sign that read 'Pierogi Ruskie'. The word 'Ruskie' was crossed out and replaced by 'Ukrainskie'. The pierogi Ruskie has a specific filling of potato and cheese and refers to an area in Ukraine that used to be called Ruthenia; thus, they are Ukrainian in origin. The language is also crucial because it would be 'Pierogi Rosyjskie' if they were Russian. But that's not what this is about, Fabio tells me. 'The seller doesn't care about all that. He has made his point clear.'

Every two and a half seconds, a pot is sold somewhere in the world.

Fabio Parasecoli is a writer and professor in the Department of Nutrition and Food Studies at New York University. He is particularly interested in the intersection between food, media and politics. 'At the beginning of the war, there was mainly a cancel culture. Russian vodka was poured away worldwide.'

Food boycotts are common. Several years ago, Matteo Salvini, the leader of the far-right Italian party, banned Nutella. Nutella is from Ferrero, a proud Italian company. Nutella is eaten worldwide, but interestingly, the contents of the famous hazelnut spread differ per country. Still, each jar has a thirteen per cent portion of hazelnuts, which is about fifty-two nuts. Every two and a half seconds, a pot is sold somewhere in the world. Annually, 365,000 tons of Nutella are produced. As you can imagine, Italy cannot grow enough hazelnuts to meet the global appetite for Nutella. Ferrero, therefore, obtains a large proportion of hazelnuts from Turkey. A thorn in the side for Matteo Salvini, who, from a nationalist perspective, believes Ferrero should only use genuine Italian nuts. But this is not an option, especially considering that Ferrero single-handedly bought a quarter of the worldwide hazelnut production in 2015. The only way for Ferrero to produce all-Italian products is to sell less, which would mean firing people or filling the whole country with hazelnuts. Probably not what Matteo would have wanted. Syrian refugees, including children, pick those Turkish hazelnuts under harsh conditions. On small hazelnut plantations with fewer than fifty employees, it is not mandatory to adhere to Turkish laws for working conditions. Surely that would be a better reason to be against Turkish hazelnuts, Matteo!

When I ask Fabio to explain how food and politics are intertwined, he explains that sometimes it starts with simple, almost banal things. Why do so many products contain glucose-fructose syrup? It's not because it's healthy; it's because we grow so much corn, making syrup a very cheap ingredient. And because it's so cheap and produced on a large scale, there is considerable power in the glucose-fructose syrup lobby. This, in turn, ensures that there are subsidies for growing corn, among other things, so that it can be produced so cheaply in the first place. And so on. 'It can be very simple, but usually, it is very complex. The food system is not an ordered system, but a complicated mishmash where logic is often lacking.'

If you want to understand the strong connection between politics and food, take something simple as a starting point. Grab a Mars bar, look it in the eye and ask it the following questions.
'Hey Mars, where are you from?
Do you come from a large supermarket?
Who works there?
How much do you cost?
What kind of jacket are you wearing?
What materials are you made from?
Do your jacket's colours have symbolic meaning?
What do the adverts for you look like?
You are made of chocolate; where does it come from?
How is the cocoa grown, and by whom?
What do fair trade and single-origin mean?
How was this cocoa transported from the plantation to the factory?
How is it processed?
What ingredients are allowed in it?
What technology is used?
Who owns the patents and rights to this technology and the brand?
Who decides which cocoa can be imported?
How is the chocolate transported?
Where does the power to advertise lie?'

These questions are only about your Mars bar. Thinking further in this way creates a picture of the influences on our everyday food – effects that you, the unsuspecting consumer, simply don't pick up on when biting into the chocolate bar.

'Hey Mars, how is your cocoa grown and by whom?
And what does fair trade mean?'

The Dutch TV series Metropolis made a programme featuring cocoa farmers in Ivory Coast. Even though the farmers had grown cocoa all their lives, they had never seen or tasted the end product because chocolate is hardly available in Ivory Coast. One part of the programme documents the moment the farmers taste chocolate for the first time. The men sit in a circle and share a bar of chocolate wrapped in a gold wrapper like a precious gift. Carefully, they break off a piece and savour the sweet flavour with blissful delight. 'That's why white people are so healthy,' one of the men declares without irony. I cringe slightly when I hear this. They have no idea that chocolate is made from their beans. Some thought the beans were used to make wine. One of the men puts the wrapper in his pocket to show his children. Another of the men says emphatically, 'What a privilege it must be to be able to eat this.'

The English diet is changing as the import of traditional ingredients becomes more difficult.

The Center for Genomic Gastronomy was founded by Cathrine Kramer and Zack Denfeld and explores human food systems from a design perspective. Brexit inspired them to develop the Brexit Banquet in collaboration with Emma Conley, Eirin Breivik and Eileen Reiner. The corresponding cuisine is inspired by traditional English dishes but with a Brexit makeover. How does Brexit affect everyday life on the island? The menu will change as the import of many conventional ingredients becomes more difficult. Fish and chips may be the first dish that comes to mind when you think of the UK. Most washed and frozen potatoes used for fish and chips come from the EU. The cod is also imported. The UK mainly exports its catch and primarily imports its food. The blue whiting, smelt and herring they catch offer an alternative, but do fish and chips made with these fish still live up to the culinary tradition?

In 2019, no less than ninety per cent of all lamb from the UK was shipped to the EU. Therefore, Cathrine and Zack propose serving lamb at every meal: breakfast, lunch and dinner. This is how people become aware of the gigantic livestock industry worth five hundred million pounds. Offal and entrails are also on the menu. These 'lesser cuts' were previously transported to Southern Europe, but that is no longer useful due to the high transportation costs. They also translated the famous English recipe 'coronation chicken' – popular because of the coronation of Queen Elizabeth II in 1953 and a symbol of the expansionism of the British Empire – into the dish 'chlorination chicken' in reference to the UK's withdrawal from EU food law. Now that the UK is no longer part of the EU, a trade agreement between the UK and the US is a possibility, as is chlorine disinfected chicken becoming widely available in supermarkets. The use of hormones, antibiotics and chemicals in the US is more widely allowed. The concern here is not only about the use of chlorine but the signal it sends to the food supply chain. Knowing that chicken is disinfected with chlorine may mean employees in the rest of the chain are less likely to observe the hygiene rules. For all Brexit Banquet dishes and recipes, visit brexitbanquet.com.

Those lamenting the changes to traditional English dishes should find solace knowing that potatoes originally grew in the Andes, sheep for lamb originally grazed in Central Asia and the mint for the sauce sprouted in the Mediterranean. Those with a nationalist streak and who oppose immigration may need to adjust their diet. I have made several dinners that address immigration. In Finland, I made an installation with Foodcamp Finland at the Olo restaurant, where guests became part of a performance. We served typical Finnish food. Apple, celery, butter, dill, pork, potato, sour cream and blueberries are ingredients that are considered traditionally Finnish. However, these are native to Central Asia, the Mediterranean, India, Egypt, China, the Andes, Eastern Europe, and North America. Each ingredient tells an invisible story in which history, politics, economy and immigration play a role.

What political message did you unsuspectingly eat for breakfast this morning?

i'll have a sandwich with additional conflict

challenge

put power on the menu

Food is power, but we are not always aware of how far that power extends. For this challenge, you will eat with a group. It can be with your family or a group of friends. The more, the better.

Prepare a large pan of food. It can be soup, a casserole or a large pan of pasta. Place the meal in the middle of the table and give everyone a plate, but put the cutlery in a heap in the middle. Also, pour a drink, and make sure you have dessert.

here are the rules for eating

-   The person with the most petite feet decides who gets cutlery and who doesn't. They can even decide only to allocate someone a knife.
-   The person who wears the most blue may exchange their cutlery with another person.
-   The person who woke up the earliest can serve themself first and as much as they want.
-   The person who did the laundry most recently gets to serve everyone but themself.
-   Anyone who has cooked the food can take a sip of everyone's drink.
-   The person who went to bed the latest may take food from someone else.
-   The person who weighs the heaviest must give half to someone else.
-   The person who cooks the most regularly may only start eating after ten minutes.
-   The person with the easiest job (what's easy?) gets a second serving.
-   If your phone number ends with a seven, you must eat everything on your plate.
-   If you have emptied your glass, you are not allowed dessert.
-   If you have not eaten any food, you can have two desserts.
-   The person who ate the most assigns another to do the dishes.
-   The person who has to do the dishes may come up with two new rules.

You can abide by the rules.
You can also negotiate.
A table of people eating is a temporary mini-state.
What happens?

the cutlery chooses you.

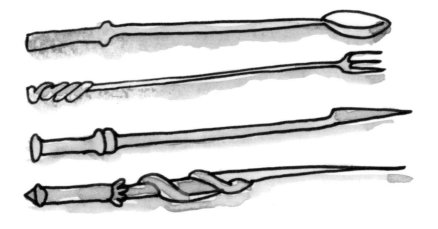

shrimp sex

Sarah looks at us with wide eyes and a wry smile on her face. 'For my graduation, I want to make sex toys. For shrimp.' On the screen behind her is an image of two white shrimp, or Litopenaeus vannamei, the most eaten shrimp in the world.

They are beautiful and complex animals with long antennae, ten tiny wobbly legs and a fascinating semi-transparent body. King prawns, their more common name, are becoming increasingly popular, even in countries where they are not usually on the menu. Wild white shrimp are native to the eastern Pacific Ocean and are bred in aquafarms off the coasts of Central America and Southeast Asia. Catching them is a destructive practice. Trawlers – fishing vessels that fish with funnel-shaped nets – are destroying the natural habitat of the shrimp and the many other animals they live with. Moreover, one kilo of shrimp produces about twenty kilos of bycatch. Shrimp farming in the ocean disrupts mangroves, the birthplace of entire ecosystems, and may even increase the risk of tsunamis. In response to this, a new development is underway: the cultivation of white shrimp on land. Shrimp are farmed in large water tanks in anonymous industrial estate warehouses. Consequently, natural ecosystems are preserved, bycatch is not an issue, and controlled cultivation requires no antibiotics. This is in contrast to aquafarms that work with nets in the open sea. Sarah Fittererr is in contact with some of the dozen German shrimp farms. 'They have already won many sustainability awards,' she chirps. She tells us how these indoor shrimp farms positively impact the ocean and how they grow antibiotic-free shrimp. It sounds like a great success. 'The only thing the farms are looking for is a way to control how shrimp reproduce.'

We usually don't think about the sex it took to make our food when we eat.

Every farmer is dependent on reproduction, whether it concerns animals or plants. Shrimp farmers are no different and count on maximum production – and production requires reproduction! In fact, most farmers are constantly busy with sex. Food is sex. Without sex, there is no food. Or, at least, a lot less. There are self-fertilising plants (see chapter Next Nature), and some animals reproduce asexually, such as salamanders and beetles, although they are not a largescale food source. Sex and food are therefore inextricably linked. When we eat, however, we usually don't think about sex. At least, not the sex it took to make our food. For example, we don't consider how animals are forced to reproduce. Many people worry about broiler chickens, but nobody wonders where the parents of broiler chickens come from or that the parents of organic chickens are often from factory farms.

Sex is also indispensable for shrimp farmers.
After all, without sex, there are no new shrimp to breed. Although indoor water tanks are a sustainable propagator, they are unfortunately not the ideal place for the picky female shrimp. Captivity causes inhibition in female shrimp, which is a problem for shrimp farmers. 'Fortunately' there is a solution. If you remove one of the female shrimp's eyestalks – pull it off, slit and crush it, cauterise it, or chemically remove it – then she wants to spawn! This eyestalk ablation produces a hormonal reaction that makes female shrimp want to reproduce like crazy. The shrimp spawns several times in succession, and, before you know it, she has laid a quarter of a million fertilised eggs. That's three times more than a shrimp with two eyes. All of this happens in an entirely predictable and almost industrial eight-day cycle.

Female shrimp don't like to do it in captivity, but they do if you pull off one of their eyes.

A Taiwanese technician discovered this at the end of the twentieth century and shared the knowledge with shrimp farmers in China, where this is still the most commonly used method for getting female shrimp to produce eggs. Indeed, in China, some people have the job of

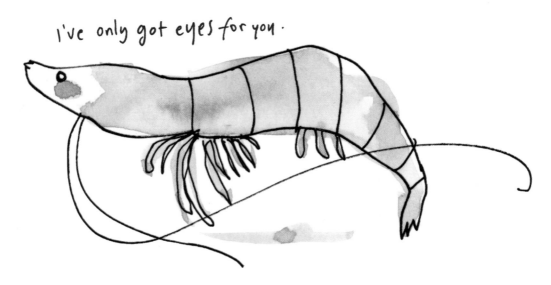

I've only got eyes for you.

depriving female white shrimp of an eye. Just like some people have the job of jerking off bulls and boars (male pigs). In Germany, it is not allowed to hurt animals 'unnecessarily'. The eyeless shrimp's larvae (the hatched eggs) are therefore sent from the US, where eyestalk ablation is permitted. The problem is that although the mother produces three times as many larvae, the larvae are much weaker. Shrimp are sensitive animals, and the larvae of the mutilated mothers need antibiotics. Many larvae will also die during the three-day transit from the US to Germany. Furthermore, they also do not fare as well as animals that have been naturally fertilised. They are smaller, more vulnerable and more prone to disease.

'If only the shrimp ladies had a higher libido, the problem would have been solved.' Sarah says this ironically because, in principle, she is against keeping animals in captivity. But for her graduation project, she put her moral preferences on hold so she could examine the situation with an open mind. It is not that the shrimp farmers weren't trying to meet the high demands of the female. Extensive research papers have been published on the reproduction of the 'Litopenaeus vannamei.' In the wild, white shrimps mate at a depth of about sixty metres in sand burrows on the seabed, preferably by moonlight. The female must be soft-shelled before she mates, so she ovulates shortly after shedding her shell, a process called moulting. She then burrows into the sand, probably because a recently moulted shrimp is vulnerable. Though mating is a moonlight affair, the ritual is usually initiated at dawn. The male swims after the female, and the couple circles around each other. Finally, the male swims under the female, turns towards her and curves around the female's body at an angle of twenty to sixty degrees, penetrating her for one to sixty seconds.

What does it take to mimic these conditions in captivity and create the right circumstances for the shrimp's lovemaking? Studies on mating behaviour are quantitative and focused on input and output. How can we adapt the situation to increase the likelihood of successful mating? Can we change the water's oxygen levels or salinity? Do shrimp prefer LED or other types of lighting? Does the water need more calcium? Is there a food that boosts libido? Some crabs are said to contain aphrodisiac hormones for shrimp. Unfortunately, after fifty years of research, there is still no ideal set-up in which white shrimp mate successfully, although good nutrition and a ratio of one male to two females certainly help. Sarah interviewed several breeders and asked them whether shrimp could fall in love. None of the respondents thought shrimp experienced love. Consciousness was also considered unlikely due to the shrimp's simple nervous system. However, Sarah spoke to a vet who takes care of one of the aqua farms and refutes this claim. 'We simply do not know. So we might as well assume that they can feel love. Given that they sometimes don't want to mate, it raises the question of whether they are feeling more than just the biological urge to reproduce when they finally get round to mating.'

What we do know is that wild shrimp do a fascinating mating dance.
The males swim in the dark depths after the females and dance in shapes on the seabed. The moonlight gives the sea a cool glow. During the dance, the female decides whether she wants to mate and with whom. There seems to be a conscious choice of partner. However, if all the reproductive indicators are fulfilled in captivity and the female still refuses to mate, is this because the right male is not present or because of the artificial environment?

The shrimp can influence their breeder with their 'sex strike'; it gives them power.

The artificial fertilisation of shrimp is not yet possible. And the shrimp's refusal to mate has an influence on themselves but also on the breeder. You could speculate that the shrimp influence the breeder through their 'sex strike'. The shrimp appear to have power. Breeders try to create the optimal conditions for the animals to increase the yield, but what if they immersed themselves in the shrimp's emotional environment, irrespective of the yield? Is it helpful for us to consider ourselves a superior species and treat the issue of shrimp sex as just a puzzle to be solved? If you map the research on 'Litopenaeus vannamei', there are many studies on its reproductive behaviour, while there is nothing to be found about social behaviour, emotions or cognitive skills. Our interest is rather one-sided, Sarah thinks.

Although she knew at the start of her graduation project that she would probably not succeed, she wanted to attempt making sex toys for shrimp. Perhaps objects the shrimp can hide behind might be helpful or 'bunk beds' made of sand because there is less space at the bottom of an indoor tank than on the seafloor. They could have rings to swim through as an accompaniment to the mating dance or water-purifying stones because clean water is one of the most important conditions for mating. The objects she creates primarily help her access the world of shrimp farming because they help her develop a conversation with the shrimp breeders. She understands it is naive to think she can solve the problem with these propositions. At the same time, she questions whether offering a solution is what she wants. Isn't she primarily seeking to challenge the idea of forced sex as a perverse act? Why do we eat shrimp when it takes so much effort to breed them? The idea that we humans will probably never fully grasp an animal's environment and motivations fascinates Sarah. However, if we make an effort, she thinks we can develop a more complex understanding of the indoor aquacultural environment. By looking beyond the technical problem, we may discover something more important. A mutual dependency exists between the shrimp and the breeder. However, the main difference is that the shrimp is dependent with its life

Sarah Fittererr | www.fittererr.com | instagram: @_fittererr

What's worse? The destruction of entire ecosystems or gouging out shrimp's eyes?

Sarah's graduation presentation features her objects hanging in a large, lifeless aquarium. She did her best to keep the shrimp she got from a breeder alive, but the animals died. She drapes the corpses on the objects, giving the presentation a forlorn appearance. The water pump provides a monotonous soundtrack. Sarah's objects were an excuse to make a documentary about the ins and outs of shrimp farming. It was not her intention to stop the consumption of shrimp. 'I can only make that choice for myself. I want us to rethink how we think about "non-humans". What makes us feel empathy for other species? I want to expose our cognitive dissonance: how we justify eating animals to ourselves, yet doing so makes us feel contradictory and uncomfortable. When does an animal get rights? At present, animals in Germany are electrocuted before slaughter which is meant to stun them first. However, the shrimp's scales are like armour, so this method does not work for them and would be unnecessarily cruel. The shrimp is a relatively new farmed species in Germany, so there is still no appropriate legislation.'

'There is no outcome,' Sarah says in her presentation. And perhaps that is how it should be. If I wrote here that Sarah had found a solution, you would probably stop thinking about it. At most, you might think, 'Great. Now I can order a guilt-free gamba 'à la plancha' at the tapas bar!' The shrimp sex story is a paradox – one of many in our food system. Paradoxes are great for revealing the normally invisible food system. It works like a contrast agent. Just like a raw shrimp is transparent at first and becomes properly visible after you have cooked it. Or is that an inappropriate comparison?

bite by bite

My mother and me walked down the kindergarten corridor. I was five years old. Back then, many mothers wore brightly coloured pantsuits. Ski suits, actually, but worn to school. My mother wore a tartan skirt with a large pin in it. I smelled an unfamiliar aroma in the school hallway. I had never smelled that aroma at school before. I didn't know what I smelled but felt the aroma almost tangibly embrace me. I hugged it back.

The aroma was creamy and warm. It was also a bit dry like paper in a book but sweeter and with a little greenery. I felt myself relax. In the hallway hung a massive piece of paper with a large brown blot on it, painted by children. I didn't know what it was supposed to be and thought the brown spot painting was stupid. It looked like a paint bucket had fallen over it. I couldn't read and only learned later that AFRICA had been painted in large children's letters. Once in class, we sat in a circle. The teacher began to talk, but my mind drifted back to that aroma, which had settled on

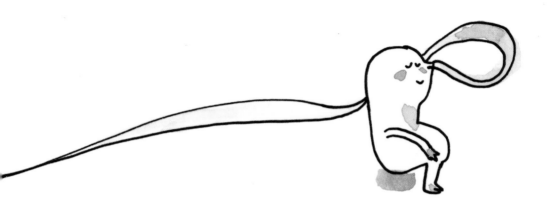

my shoulders like a soft blanket. 'Hello, sweet aroma,' I whispered. The teacher looked earnestly around the circle, seeking our gaze with intense eyes. 'And that's not nice,' she said with her jarring tone. I was sorry I didn't know what the conversation concerned. Maybe it would help if I also looked serious and nodded. The mothers in the class – hip mothers with wild hair and smelling of LouLou – also looked earnest. The teacher told us we could now experience how bad it was. Thanks in part to the mothers' help.

The aroma intensified and summoned me from the other room.

As the door to the adjacent classroom opened, the aroma intensified. It summoned me from the other room. Pans of steamed rice with warm vapour swirling above them sat on the tables. 'Today, you will experience how difficult it is to eat dry rice without any sauce, just like those poor children in Africa.' One of the mothers said decisively, kneeling at our height. 'Those poor children don't have any cutlery, so you must eat the rice with your hands,' she added. I got a scoop of steaming grains. We were allowed to form the rice into balls. I ate the rice gratefully from my infant hand. 'This is the best day of my life,' I mused happily.

My gratitude came from pure pleasure.
It did not come from the realisation that I was living a privileged life, as the eighties mothers tried to instil in me. They did so with good intentions but a misplaced sense of cultural respect. I envied the kids in Africa, regardless of who they were. Though my compassion for distressed

children was hard to find that day, my profound love for rice was palpable. This love has been imprinted deep onto my being ever since. As I write this, I feel incredibly uncomfortable with the stereotyping of an entire continent and the condescending way development aid was viewed at the time. As children in the 1960s, my parents were also told to empty their plates and 'think about the children going hungry in Africa.' Making something tangible can be an effective teaching tool, but it has to fit within your frame of reference.

The watercress werewolf

Juni was two or three years old. A sweet, cheerful chatterbox with big blue eyes and an energetic body. At the time, she was my first and only child. No matter how happy and affable she played, every day, she would quickly transform from a cute little toddler into an evil monster, like a werewolf during a daylight full moon. Something would change in her eyes. At first, they looked open and happy at the world, but when I pushed the high chair to the table, her stare darkened to announce an incoming storm. The dining table, which moments before was a joyful finger-painting studio, became a bleak battleground. She didn't immediately start to scream. Her tactics were more sophisticated. She would wait until I, already cautious, put the food on the table. Children that age are not given much influence over their lives. They are picked up and taken to grandpa's, kindergarten, or the shop. They are plonked in the shower and then dressed. A child can reverse this balance of power by simply not opening its mouth when it's time to eat. It is a wonderful moment for the child. By refusing food, especially vegetables, Mom will do all sorts of funny things, such as singing songs and cutting the food into small pieces of 'vegetable flowers'. There's also the talking green beans and the angry words and pleas.

The essential tools for making the jewels were their own sharp teeth.

Although I understood my daughter's temperament, it frustrated me enormously. I would rather have healthy eating habits than a healthy attitude! I discovered two things. Firstly, I had apparently allowed the Pavlov effect to develop as a young mother, so when I sat my daughter at the table, she assumed her forbidding assertiveness in advance. Secondly, I read that a child has to taste a new flavour at least seven times to accept it. It's a bit like learning a new language: you only learn new words through repetition. My darling monster was already very hesitant, and I had no idea how to make her taste the same thing seven times. Once was already a challenge. So I devised a cunning plan. I held a 'Veggie bling bling' workshop at my studio and invited all the children from her day care centre. Vegetables filled the large table in the middle of the room. I told the toddlers that they were going to make jewellery and their tools would be their own teeth. Children's teeth are small yet very sharp and are perfect for gnawing. I also provided some cookie cutters and a drill for making holes in carrots.

Here's a nice tip if you try this yourself:
Drill a hole lengthways through a few carrots from the thick end.
Stick the children's fingers into the carrots. This magical witch's hand is fun to
play with and can be shaped on the hand into wands or swords.

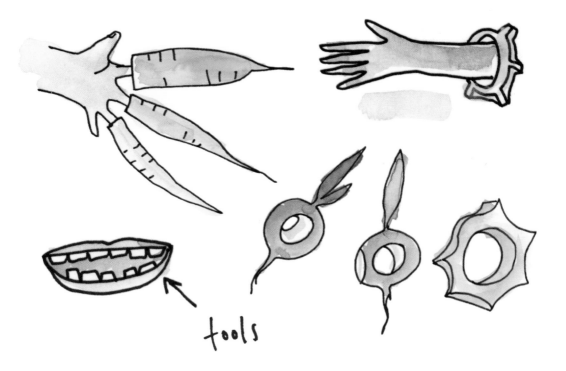

tools

The children rushed to the table and quickly began playing because what they encountered was
not food; it was play. They put the vegetables into their mouths and frantically shaped the jewels
with their teeth. The children forgot about their suspicion of vegetables, so no one spat anything
out. Everything that was chewed off was swallowed. Naturally, they were playing, not eating. Each
ring, bracelet or necklace was beautifully gnawed into shape as they tasted, tasted and tasted
– more than seven times. A little boy, with a clump of tousled brown hair and red blushes, had
gotten up and stood a few steps from the table, staring dreamily into the sky. On his wrist hung
the beet bracelet he had made. He gnawed a nice shape into it, holding his arm in the air, daydreaming and forgetting what he was doing. He gnawed and gnawed until his bracelet was gone.

Little Juni had a good time. From that moment on, I noticed a remarkable difference in her approach to vegetables when eating at home. Of course, she didn't suddenly like everything, but she tasted new things more adventurously and with more pleasure. I heard the same from other parents. In addition to the different settings, from the dining table to the workshop table, and tasting the vegetables more than seven times, the positive peer pressure also contributed. Children would much rather try things out with their friends than with their stupid parents.

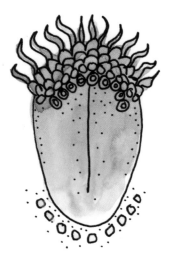

For parents of young children, this experience can profoundly affect daily life. But its effect can be even more significant and impactful. 'We change the world through our taste buds!' Susanne Høljund Pedersen exclaimed as she held up an enlarged felt taste bud, resembling some sort of flower pod from the movie Avatar. I was speaking for the second time at the Creative Tastebuds conference in Denmark. What Susanne, the driving force behind the conference, meant by this became apparent during the sessions with behavioural psychologists, anthropologists, political scientists, chefs and other food experts. The bottom line is that we can learn to enjoy sustainable food, making it easier to live more sustainably. (See chapter Good.)

Bee Wilson's face appeared on a large screen. She was unable to attend in person due to the pandemic. Bee is a food writer, and in her book, 'First Bite', she explains that our eating preferences are primarily learned, not innate. She believes this is the key to a better world. I spoke to Bee, and she told me about her TastEd programme for schools: taste education instead of food education. 'If food is taught in schools at all, it is usually about the food itself and cooking techniques. Only a small number of ingredients are included. But taste education is about how you experience food, such as smell, sound, mouthfeel and playing. Taste education helps children and adults to expand their gustative experience. You must learn how to eat before learning how to cook.' You probably think everyone already knows how to eat, so this might sound a little unusual. In the UK, where Bee works, one in five primary school children is overweight, and one in three is still overweight when they leave primary school. You may think those children should get healthier food, but they have access to healthy food regularly. Very often, the children, and their parents, simply do not like healthy food. The idea that good food is unhealthy and that healthy food is unpleasant seems to be deeply ingrained in many people's minds. When a new product is described as 'healthy', test subjects find it less tasty than when it is labelled as 'new'. Many adults try to eat more vegetables because it's the healthy option, but they don't bother to ensure they actually enjoy them. And the latter is the key to wanting to eat healthy more often.

The food industry's holy grail is the 'bliss point', the ideal ratio of sweet, salty and fat.

It doesn't help that avoiding unhealthy food is more challenging nowadays. A lot of cheap, unhealthy food is developed to have an addictive effect because it triggers a response in our brain. Food technologists and psychologists call this the 'bliss point': the blissful feeling that occurs from the ideal ratio of sweet, salt and fat in one hit (er ... bite). It's the food industry's holy grail because, once the bliss point is reached, hardly anyone can resist eating a tub or bag of the orgasmic product in one go. However, not everyone is susceptible to the addictive effects of this combination. In her book, Bee unravels the processes that lead to developing personal flavour preferences. Although research results show that small children in an isolated situation make 'healthy' choices, they are not spared 'real world' influences. Whereas the study only made tests using a selection of unprocessed food, a lot of processed food is available in normal daily circumstances. The test results would likely have been different with the inclusion of processed food. Moreover, we do not live in an isolated situation. From an early age, we are constantly confronted with advertisements and the food inclinations of those around us.

In their book, 'Eating Like Animals', David Raubenheimer and Stephen J. Simpson explain that though animals have no conscious knowledge of nutrition, they always adopt a diet that balances proteins and carbohydrates whether or not they are omnivores. Provided they have access to enough food, of course. In this sense, we are all hard-wired to eat the right thing. So, why don't we? The two scientists explain that the body associates salty flavours with protein. However, protein is expensive. Therefore, the food industry makes cheap carbohydrates taste like salt. Your body registers protein but gets sugar and fat. Bee also concludes that we may have an innate predisposition to eat the right foods, but we no longer live in a natural nutritional environment. Therefore, how we handle food and what we choose to eat is more learned than innate. Take coffee and wine, for example. Many adults never thought of drinking coffee as a child, but now they can't live without it. The principle of an 'acquired taste' can also be applied to health. Pleasure and health go hand in hand. You can teach yourself to enjoy healthy food. Throughout your life, you have also learned to dislike certain things.

You can teach yourself to like different flavours and healthy food.

Food industrialisation is also not helping. The more standardised food you eat, the more difficult it becomes to try new food because you grow accustomed to unvarying flavours. If you only eat ready-made lasagne, you are less likely to be open to the taste of fresh homemade lasagne. If we think something 'should taste' a certain way, it becomes increasingly difficult to accept a different variety. Knowing you can train your taste buds can help you take matters into your own hands. If you follow a diet thinking, 'I can't eat anything I like,' you won't last long. You can transform your constraint into abundance when you realise that taste preference is a learnable skill. In countries where people eat a lot of chilli, such as in much of Asia, Africa and South America, the children are not born with a predilection for chilli. Nor are people in these countries less sensitive to chilli. Children in these lands hardly eat spicy food before age five. The big difference with countries where little chilli is eaten is the way it is spoken about. Adults in much of Asia and Africa say they think food without chilli is bland. Chilli brings a taste sensation, excitement and adventure. When children are allowed to season their food, they follow their family's taste preferences.

I once ate with Bas Valckx from the Dutch Embassy in Tokyo. I asked him which Japanese dishes he did not like. To the Dutch, some Japanese dishes seem otherworldly. Bas, who has lived in Japan for a long time, laughed. 'I've decided to like and eat everything,' he replied. 'If a country has eaten the food for countless years and the people can live on it, isn't it arrogant not to eat or like it?' Since my conversation with Bas, I also eat and like everything. Maybe the food isn't to my immediate liking, but I know I can train myself to like it. Being curious about everything vastly enriches your life because your senses experience more adventures, and you expand your taste palette. It is like having many more colours in your paint box.

Knowing that you can positively influence your taste preferences can be the foundation for a healthier world. How we experience flavour affects our brains. Our brains are flexible and continuously adapt. For example, if you decide to stop eating sugar, it can be challenging for the first few days. But, ultimately, your sugar craving will adapt to your intake. You become more sensitive and therefore need less sugar to experience sweetness. As such, you can play with your taste perception. This can cause you to no longer like sweet and salty industrial food. You can reprogram your brain and taste buds by taking a two-week 'vacation' away from your old gustation patterns. Liking or disliking something's flavour often seems trivial, so we usually pay it little attention. However, looking back on your life, you will see that your taste was never fixed. Your taste preferences change, even though you never consciously controlled this. But what would happen if you did? Bite by bite.

challenge

I. eat yourself rich (3+)

I have taken the Veggie bling bling workshop all over the world, including to the MAD Food-camp in Copenhagen and the Victoria and Albert Museum in London. And now it's coming to your home!

veggie bling bling workshop

Invite a group of children from the age of three upwards. Tell them that they are going to make their own vegetable jewellery. Make sure you use words that are about play, not food. Choose raw vegetables that are easy to shape for the base. Root vegetables, such as daikon radish, yellow, white and red beetroot (Chioggia beets are wonderful), thick carrots, celeriac, kohlrabi and large radishes work well. Pumpkin, courgettes or bell peppers are also good. However, potatoes and aubergines are not suitable raw.

Provide cutting boards, small knives, a cookie cutter and an apple corer. Depending on the age and size of the group, you will need adults to help cut vegetables. Tell the children they will make jewellery and shape it with their teeth and show them how it is done. Jewellery can be all kinds of things. You can make earrings, nose rings, necklaces, crowns, swords and wands. You can easily create a bracelet by cutting a hole in a slice of a root vegetable large enough for a child's hand to fit through. Put it on and gnaw away!

Take pictures of the gnawing and the jewellery and share them on instagram: **@lickit.book** Collect all the cut pieces of vegetables and make soup from them.

2. teach yourself new flavours

Write down one ingredient you don't like and want to learn to eat. Find someone who also finds particular foods unpleasant and get them to join you – a taste buddy.

ingredient:

name taste buddy and their ingredient:

step 1
Decide that you like the ingredient, even if you don't yet.

step 2
Eat one bite of the ingredient for seven days. You can prepare it differently each day; it doesn't have to be much. Write down how you prepared it and what the tasting experience was like.

1

2

3

4

5

6

7

Send a daily photo to your taste buddy to show you are tasting the food.

stap 3
After a week, prepare and eat dinner together with both ingredients and conclude that you are heroic and sexy. Why sexy? Just because you can.

animism

Do you want the red or the blue pill? Neo looks at Morpheus and doesn't need long to decide: he takes the red pill and, in doing so, sees how the Matrix really works. The pill itself is quite boring; it doesn't do or say anything. If I were that red pill, I'd say, 'Hey, sexy Keanu Reeves, put me on your lips! Lick me gently with your tongue before you swallow me. Let me take a look around your body to see if you're as sexy on the inside as you are on the outside.' The pill has a massive effect in the film, but it is no more than a functional object.

Will you choose the seed in my left hand or the one in my right hand? You put the grain – to which I gave a voice in an audio guide for an exhibition – in your mouth. He yells, 'Hey! Show me the inside of your mouth! I want to explore all the bumps on your tongue but also slide between your teeth and the inside of your upper lip. Come, show me around!' You do as he asks and let him slide down the outside of your lower teeth as well. It's funny that you never do anything with this part of your mouth despite it always being there. The seed howls, 'what a great ride!' and tells you it's time to swallow him. He shrieks as he slides down the chute to your stomach. You don't feel the seed anymore. It's strange that you can't feel food after swallowing it, even though it's still in your body. Luckily you can still hear it. The seed swims around in the pool of your stomach. In the meantime, you walk to the next part of the exhibition, where grain is being ground.

The seed sobs, distressed at seeing other grains crushed. But he also sees the beauty in grain being ground for bread, the staple food for so many people. Still, you feel relief when you move to the next part of the exhibition, where both you and the seed learn a lot more about just how magical a seed actually is.

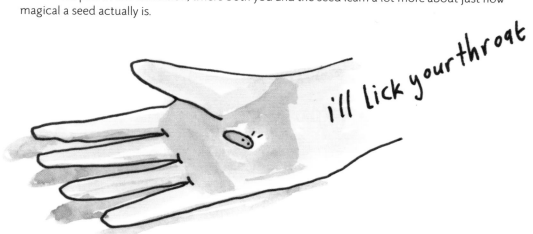

i'll lick your throat

Animism is when we attribute objects, food, plants and places a soul.

There is evidence that most people's beliefs were animistic prior to the emergence of monotheistic and polytheistic religions. Animism is a philosophical concept in which a living soul is not only attributed to people and animals but also to things, plants and rivers. Animism still plays a role in various cultures. In Japan, for example, sewing workshops often have a small shrine to all the broken needles. December 8 in eastern Japan or February 8 in western Japan is the 'Day of the Broken Needles', when the past year's broken needles and pins are laid to rest by pricking them in tofu blocks.

Shintoism holds that our tools absorb the user's frustration, and on their hundredth 'birthday', they transform into monsters called 'tsukumogami'. Dolls and other figures with eyes and human characteristics also have souls and cannot simply be thrown away. They must be treated with respect. If you return the doll to a temple, where they perform a special ritual with the toy, it can depart from this world without negative consequences

You probably do not believe in animism yourself, but you may have done so as a child. Did you ever yell 'stupid door!' when you stubbed your toe against it as if the door intentionally hurt you? Maybe, like me, you thought it was sad that the 'baby pepper' was separated from its mother while cooking and eating it. Nowadays, you seldom see those mini peppers growing inside another bell pepper. (See chapter Next Nature.) What does it mean when things around you have a soul? What if the book you're now holding has a soul? What was the paper before it became this book? Perhaps it was once wiped buttocks or had divorces recorded on it. Would it still carry that energy? Or does it carry the energy of my stories? I hope it's a curious book. A book that asks you: 'Hey .... (insert your name), why are you reading? Go outside, where real life happens!'

Animism can help free you from your perspective and see things from a different point of view. However, you can never fully step out of your particular situation and into someone else's, so you can never fully grasp what life is like for something or someone else. Though, it would be very nice to be a dairy cow for a week. I would learn a lot from this, despite the fact I would probably be a rather grumpy cow. Yet, even after a week, I would still be unable to comprehend the cow's perspective fully. I am human. The moment you imagine things have a soul, you treat them with more respect. We humans try to be considerate of other people and our 'preferred animals', such as dogs, cats and cute garden birds. We prefer to see lice, wasps and processionary caterpillars exterminated. (Incidentally, designer Emile Corre makes a sauce from fermented processionary caterpillars). Chickens, pigs and cows are production livestock and serve as consumer goods, but without their consent. We use or transform plants, stones and rivers when it suits us. To us, refrigerators, mopeds and toothbrushes are nothing more than meaningless things without a voice. We use them and throw them away when we no longer need them. If your toothbrush did have a soul, you would probably be less likely to throw it away. You would keep it well cleaned and never miss a brush, or he might feel ignored. And who wants to brush their teeth with a sad toothbrush that might cry in your mouth? If your toothbrush tastes salty, then you know something is wrong. Give your toothbrush more attention!

I summoned the bento spirit into being; maybe it can revive the 'old-fashioned' Bento box.

I find Japanese animism inspiring. I once made an exhibition in Tokyo about the bento box. In Japan, this is not merely a lunch box but a deeply rooted cultural phenomenon. According to the Shinto religion, some objects come to life after a hundred years and receive a soul. But there are also 'gods' and 'spirits'. There is a spirit of rice, a spirit of wagashi (traditional sweets) and a spirit of the toilet. But how could I, as a non-Japanese person, tell the Japanese something new about bento with my exhibition? Maybe I didn't have to. I wanted to create space for a new perspective and the discovery of unseen properties of bento. While many products and spaces are assigned a spirit in Japan, there is no bento spirit. So I created one. It is small, white as rice, fits in your lunch box, and wears a hat made from umeboshi, dried pickled plum.

The bento spirit awaits you when you visit the exhibition. You can see him through a magnifying glass sitting in the bento box. He takes you with him and shows you the unseen aspects of bento. People's memories of their mother or father's bento, for example. Or the bento that they lovingly prepared for their children. Visitors walk through a materialised monument of memories and also note down their own. The bento spirit shows you that modern bento is usually sold ready-made and excessively packaged, especially in big cities. This creates a colossal mountain of waste. If you genuinely believe that everything has a soul, would you throw away so much plastic? Would you treat your things and the environment so carelessly? In Japan, everything is individually wrapped like beautiful gifts, making what's inside seem more valuable. However, the resulting waste does not justify this practice. The bento spirit then shows you that the solution lies in the old-fashioned bento box, which often contains leftovers from the previous day. Perhaps it will be easier to bring the old-fashioned bento back to life if the bento spirit is by your side and present in the lunch box. Look, there he is. Give him a wave!

The seed – from the beginning of this story – is really in your body. I used this fact when I made an installation for the Canadian company Caesarstone. Visitors received an audio guide and listened to the seed speak. You hand in the audio guide when you leave the installation, but you might still hear the voice of the seed echoing in your head. For example, if you go to the toilet, he calls out from the bowl, 'Why did you poop me out indoors and not outside? At least there I can grow again!' By giving the seed a voice and listening to it, you pause for a moment and contemplate the wonder of it all.

Maybe it will help you to feel more respect and connection with food.

The seed and the bento spirit are examples of how animism can help find a different perspective. They help you feel more reverence and connection with food in a light way. Didactic sermons about having respect for something or someone are counterproductive for me. But when the food speaks for itself, I feel empathy. Giving food a part in the theatre of life changes how you look at it and allows you to take on a different role. Who says you always have to be yourself? For a Dutch Design Week exhibition about the future of food, I asked visitors to choose between the role of consumer or producer. Depending on the choice, they were given a completely different story for exactly the same works. (See chapter Backwards.) Taking on a different role, however subtle, triggers different thinking. This was evident during dinner at my restaurant Proef, where we made corsages with names. Upon arrival, the guests received an edible flower on a sticker bearing a random name. Anita was Serge all evening, Wim transformed into Lucas, and Laetitia became Jack for the sitting. It affected the guests. They felt slightly different as Guillermo than as Sylvia, and it was also a great icebreaker. It very subtly influenced the part each guest played for the night.

But what if you are not the eater but the food?
A few years ago, students drove my colleagues and me in a supermarket cart through a dark corridor of an old industrial building in Eindhoven for a 'dinner of the future'. The starter consisted of a glass vessel with two holes, which contained mosquitoes. You were a donor to a mosquito restaurant for the appetiser, sticking your arms into the container to feed the little vampires.

How rigid we often are in our role as diners. Would it hurt to imagine your apple squealing as you peel it? Would it be wrong to play a voracious carnivore for one day when you are actually a pure vegan? (It's odd that people say they 'are' something. Wouldn't it be better to talk from the principles you 'have'?) What would you discover if you become someone or something else for a while? Tonight I'm Josephine. I suspect she eats very differently than I do. She is very prim and proper and nibbles from a small spoon. Well, apparently, that's what I think about Josephines. I'm going to do it and ask Mark to call me Josephine tonight. She probably wants champagne too.

challenge

eat like someone else

Most people are creatures of habit. So am I! I have a favourite cup for my coffee, which I take out of the dishwasher dirty if necessary and wash it by hand. I always brush my teeth with my right hand, and I always put on my right sock first. If I go to a restaurant where I have eaten something I liked before, I will choose it again next time. I think this is very stupid of me because I like to consider myself an adventurous eater. In reality, I'm not that much more advanced than Sheldon Cooper from The Big Bang Theory.

Someone from the marketing department of Albert Heijn, a Dutch supermarket chain, once told me that, even though an average supermarket has thousands of products on display, a consumer buys on average no more than a hundred different products and keeps choosing from that range. Professor of Neuropsychology Erik Scherder says that the same daily routines cause your brain to age faster. Challenging yourself creates more brain plasticity, even with small tasks like brushing your teeth with the other hand or eating with your hands instead of cutlery. Since brain plasticity helps creative thinking, you can arrive at new ideas or unexpected solutions faster if you keep challenging yourself.

This challenge invites you to take on a different 'eating avatar' for three days. Choose a personality each day and only eat what you think corresponds to it. Choose products and dishes that you normally don't eat that often. Give each day's avatar a name, or go one step further and dress differently for the day. You could use different crockery or adopt another way of eating. Perhaps as a 'petite' person, you only eat with cocktail sticks for the day, or you could be 'meticulous' with carefully weighed portions. Maybe you could talk with an accent or suddenly crave eating wildly and messily.

Write down your experiences in the food diary below and share it on instagram: @lickit.book

avatar optie

petit	meticulous	badass ninja
don't give a damn	kid	wild
sexy	granny	create your own avatar:

day 1

name avatar

breakfast

lunch

dinner

findings

day 2

name avatar

breakfast

lunch

dinner

findings

day 3

name avatar

breakfast

lunch

dinner

findings

hunger

I put my hand in my mouth. I've washed it first, and it smells like soap. Slowly, I edge my hand in further. Once past my mouth, I continue, reaching deeper and deeper until my elbow is in my throat and my hand arrives in my stomach. There, I uncurl my fingers and beckon to Hunger.

Hunger already knows what is about to happen. He crouches in the corner of my stomach and looks startled at my hand. I beckon again. Little by little, hunger comes closer. He carefully crawls onto my hand, which I close gently around him as if he were a chick. I don't want to crush him, but I don't want him to escape. I remove my hand from my throat and look intently at my fist as I carefully open it. Hunger peeks at me with big, kind eyes. He is a shadow, weightless. He seems a little scared. I reassure him. 'There's no need to be scared. I'm curious about you,' I say softly. Then I hold him to my ear. He whispers that he is not afraid of me and tells me he thought I'd be frightened of him. 'Most people are afraid of me,' he says sadly. 'They don't want to feel me. As soon as I arrive, if only for a moment, they want to crowd me out as quickly as possible.'

Hunger airs his heart.
'I have no ill intentions. I am part of life. I'm not necessarily bad. I can also be beneficial when tamed. If you cultivate me, I can even make you healthier. But if I grow too big, I could kill you. I can grow like a wild beast and tear you apart. Whatever you think of me, I've always been part of you people. In this time of plenty, you seem to want to kill me. But I do not blame you. I'm not like you. I always come back.'

Hunger prompts me to take a deep breath and imagine my air-filled stomach is a sun whose rays reach all over my body. 'Do you feel yourself?' he asks. 'You are made of billions of cells. All your cells renew and grow, a process that never stands still. Your cells can mutate, get old and get sick. Do you ever take the time to clean up those cells, to clean yourself, like how you brush your teeth, so that you have less chance of infections? I can do that. Actually, I am similar to food. Eating can make you better when you are sick, but it can also make you sick when you are healthy. I, too, can make you both sick and healthy. Though many people think hunger is useless, I am as necessary as your food. I'm like a piece of music in which the silences add a sense of tension and make the subsequent sounds even more overwhelming. A silence or pause is not "nothing". A pause creates space – space to recover and calibrate. However, people only focus on sound. They mainly recognise silence as the absence of sound. The same is true of hunger, except the absence is food. But these contrasts are necessary! Indeed, what if there was only light and no darkness? Then we wouldn't be able to see anything.'

'We need emptiness. It makes way for new things.'

'Just blink your eyes,' Hunger says sweetly. 'You see? We also need emptiness. Emptiness makes way for new things. It makes way for new cells, a new outlook, a new appreciation or a new flavour sensation. Did you know I also shape your taste? I allow you to experience things differently. I am deadly. I am strong and sharp. I am part of life. Nourish me. Cultivate me. Think of me as a super-power, but don't let me grow too big. I would be sorry if I were to lose you.' Finally, Hunger kisses my ear, and a shiver runs through me. I was thinking of a currant bun with cheese. It was time. I had filled my days and emptied my body.

I am not a big fan of currant buns. Now, with the first bite, I thank Hunger with my thoughts. Because of him, my currant bun with cheese is now the most orgasmic food on earth.

Ouroboros

There are other things I love much more than a currant bun with cheese, but curiously, I kept craving them. So, I resolved to eat a currant bun with cheese when I was going to break my fast – the literal meaning of breakfast. I ate nothing for five days and drank only water, tea and coffee. When fasting, you discover that if you do not eat anything, EVERYTHING becomes about food. You think about food, smell food and notice how much more time you have when you don't eat. You experience what it is like to prepare food for your family without tasting it. I should also mention that fasting is a luxury for me because I know that I can take a bite of the food that is always all around me. During the fast, I didn't have to worry about when I would eat again: that makes all the difference between fasting and starvation.

In the past, hunger was a natural part of life, with periods of scarcity and of abundance.

When you fast for a while, your body starts eating its waste cells, a process called ketosis. You become like the serpent in the ouroboros, an ancient symbol depicting a snake eating its tail. Ketosis gives you a kind of sickly mouth odour. (See chapter Smell.) I wonder if the ouroboros serpent's mouth also stinks. Our bodies need ketosis to clean up. By continually eating, we deny our body the chance to get rid of 'old' cells. In ancient times, hunger was a natural part of life. There were times of scarcity and of abundance. While the hunger shouldn't last too long, it also has a cleansing effect. Most of humanity now lives in overwhelming abundance, and, for many, hunger is an exception. That blessing has a downside if you don't occasionally allow your body a break from the constant eating, digesting and defecating. Our bodies are more resistant to malnutrition than abundance. There are indications that fasting may help with chemotherapy because it causes the body to start clearing itself. Fasting is an annual ritual in most religions. The spiritual challenge is paramount, but I imagine the physical benefits were also known in earlier times.

During my fasting period, I wanted to connect with the hunger in my stomach. Or was the hunger actually nestling in my head? What exactly is hunger? Hunger is an uncomfortable feeling we generally dislike. We want to take away the discomfort. But what if you surrender to the malaise and relax in the process? After all, it's just a sensation. It's not bad for your body to fast for a short time. It's uncomfortable, and we seem less and less resistant to it. Perhaps that's what I find most interesting about fasting: learning to deal with the discomfort. It starts with an observation: 'hello, hunger!' And then you embrace the feeling and ease into the situation. It is an exercise in acceptance and letting go.

Fasting taught me much about how we live now, with as much comfort as possible as the goal. If you are hungry, then you eat. If you are cold, then you put the heating on. And if you want to see a good movie, almost everything is available on demand. In Noah Yuval Harari's book 'Sapiens', he writes about 'the comfort trap'. He explains that pursuing an easier life also brings unexpected challenges. Growing food and living in one place initially seemed more manageable than being a nomadic hunter-gatherer. Still, it eventually led to a hard life marked by disease, disputes over land ownership, power struggles, envy and all the accompanying conflicts. A supermarket full of affordable and delicious food from around the world may seem like a land of plenty, but it brings obesity and indifference. Comfort appears to be an end in itself and more important than health, a meaningful life or personal development.

I discussed this with Pius Tschumi, curator of the exhibition 'Hunger' at the Museum Mühlerama in Zurich. 'We have to make sure people get hungry again!' he exclaims in surprise. Then explains, 'I heard this bizarre statement from a prominent person in the bread industry. He said this because he wanted to sell more bread but was reaching the limit of how much you could sell to the same number of consumers. Do we really want people to get hungry again? And what exactly is hunger? The question fascinated me, and it's why I made this exhibition.'

Worldwide there are about as many overweight people as those living in hunger.

'Hunger is a brilliant and complicated subject. It evokes harrowing scenes of famine in distant lands. We were therefore concerned that people wouldn't visit the exhibition, because acute starvation isn't exactly a popular topic. Of course, it's part of the exhibition, but it's not the main subject. I am particularly fascinated in showing hunger's manifestations, even in wealthy countries. Humanity has always lived with hunger. Our current era is the first in history where such a large part of Earth's population never experiences hunger. In fact, many people routinely overeat. Worldwide there are about as many overweight people as those living in hunger. Yet malnourishment exists in both groups. You can be overweight and still not get enough nutrients. You can even be obese and experience hunger. You see this phenomenon in some parts of the US, where it often affects the socially disadvantaged.'

The exhibition shows a video called 'Death Recipe' by spoken word artist Erica McMath Sheppard. You see Erica, an overweight, African American teenage woman who recites: 'We eat like we still slaves [...] Family functions we got that kill your soul food.' She vocalises about her relatives with type 2 diabetes and her uncle, who slowly went blind and lost his foot through amputation. She voices how her nine-year-old nephew gets insulin injections from his mother and about her five-year-old brother, who has juvenile diabetes. She tells about her struggle with sugar. She knows it is not right, but her whole family is addicted to sugar, and their diet is the only one they know. She rhythmically lists the ingredients that make up her food. 'Sugar, high fructose corn syrup, hydrogenated oils, whey powder, dye yellow 40, dye 52.' Then she intones, 'dye, dye, dye' as if the food itself is screaming that it is terrible for you and will kill you.

Fast food dominates and fresh food is scarce in American food deserts.

Erica is representative of many Americans who slide into a suffocating diet because of poverty and crippling cultural and geographical circumstances. Erica lives in San Francisco, where McDonald's restaurants are only found in socially deprived neighbourhoods. Such areas are called food deserts: places where fast food is cheap and readily available and fresh food is relatively expensive and difficult to obtain. In these places, you often see families struggling with their income, and the markets with fresh, healthy food are usually miles away. Fast food is not nourishing, and it makes you tired. And the more physically tired you are, the more effort it takes to break the vicious circle. Conditions like these, where children have obesity, type 2 diabetes and fat and sugar addictions, can also be called 'hunger'. The body is in a constant state of panic, seeking satiation and becomes just as tired as someone who is hungry. You may think these situations only occur in the US, but obesity and type 2 diabetes are growing global problems. Hunger, in all its forms, is, unfortunately, mostly a political topic and often has little to do with food itself.

'Our ancestors had an obsession with the land of plenty,' says Pius. 'They told stories to one another and made paintings about that special time that might one day come, where roasted pigeons fly into your mouth. Most of the population now lives in this state of plenty, but we seem to ascribe increasingly less value to it, whereas one would expect gratitude. When food is cheap, we become indifferent and waste more and more of it. We throw away no less than fifty-four per cent of bread.' Pius wonders whether we could cultivate a new desire. 'What can we long for now if there is no real hunger? If we now live in the once glorified land of plenty, should we formulate a new ideal for the future?'

Instead of gratitude, we are indifferent and waste more and more food.

An extreme version of the land of milk and honey might be the Korean phenomenon of mukbang. These eating videos usually feature a slender, beautiful young woman who films herself, as if sitting opposite you, eating large quantities of food. We love to watch people eat. Even cooking programmes where you can't smell or taste anything have very high viewing figures, often without the viewers cooking what they see in the show. The food fantasy has us in its grip, but so has its social aspect. 'That's the funny thing about hunger,' Pius continues, 'you get hungry every day. Every day the desire for food reawakens. As such, our exhibition is not only about hunger as a world problem but also as a sensation. Hunger can thus be a seed for the imagination – an emptiness that provides space for something else. We may be satisfied when fully stuffed, but the scope for fantasy and challenge is lacking.'

challenge

five days, one colour

What is it like having choices?
And what is it like having no choices?
Hunger is not simply about malnutrition or a lack of food; it's also about the absence of something and the consequent craving for it. To present a fasting or detox challenge here seemed uninspiring. You can always do that yourself, and I highly recommend it.
This challenge is about understanding the power of colour. You will discover what happens when you eat only one colour for five days. Will you get colour hunger? Or will you be inspired to find more variation within one colour?

instructions

Start these five days by choosing one colour from the list.

brown
orange
yellow
black
green
red
purple
white

Your chosen colour will be your diet for the next five days.
From the moment you start this challenge, you will only eat this colour food for every meal!
You are not allowed to eat other colours, but you can be creative with your chosen colour.
Are white asparagus white or yellow?

Prepare a day in advance so you can start with your breakfast immediately. Put a reminder on your phone so you are not unexpectedly faced with a colourful meal. Write your experience of each meal below and take a picture of everything.
Share your photos on instagram: **@lickit.book**

blocks

What was your absolute favourite dessert when you were eight years old? Maybe it was your grandmother's homemade zabaglione, slow-cooked crema catalana or pavlova. For me, the ultimate luxurious dessert was something we only ate once a year at Christmas.

I would look forward to it for days. And though I was always stuffed from the other highlight – gourmetten – there was always room for this. ('Gourmetten' became popular in the Netherlands in the 1970s and involves a tabletop stove for cooking meat, usually in little raclette pans.) I am, of course, talking about the Viennetta ice cream dessert! The white block of vanilla ice cream with ripples, ruffles and wafer-thin, crunchy layers of chocolate that makes a cracking sound when you scrape off small pieces with your spoon. I would eat it with the smallest spoon to make the enjoyment last as long as possible and push the layers apart with my tongue. My brother and I argued over who had the largest slice, but each piece was, in fact, too small. 'When I grow up, I'll work hard and save up so I can buy myself a whole Viennetta!' I always thought. To my younger self, it was the most luxurious and special dessert in the world. I also thought itwas very expensive. I just looked online to see how much they cost today in 2022. One whole vanilla brick will currently set you back roughly three euros. That's about as much as a cappuccino to go.

Now that I'm an adult, I could build a Viennetta igloo if I wanted.

And I can take bites here and there at random, wearing only underpants. I could watch my wonderful vanilla-scented dome begin to melt. The ruffles would soon lose their definition and drift sadly downwards. The chocolate centre lasts a little longer, though. But gradually, dark brown shards would be floating perilously in a thick, pale sludge. I imagine two love-struck, shivering ants clinging desperately to a chocolate cliff edge, portraying the ironic tragedy of drowning in sweet cream in a perfect Titanic moment. 'I'll never let go!' I could build that igloo, but I'll resist the temptation out of compassion for the ants.

The layered ice cream cake was conceived in 1981 and promoted as the ultimate Christmas dessert: one in ten Dutch people now eat it at Christmas.

The Viennetta ice cream dessert is a prime example of a sophisticated industrial product: it is cheap to make and ingeniously designed. Mechanical manufacture makes it possible to stack endless, delicately thin layers of chocolate with ice cream in between without becoming too expensive. Making a Viennetta involves piping ice cream onto a conveyor belt that runs slower than the ice cream's extrusion speed. This process results in a 'concertina effect' of recognisable ripples. These cheerful undulations simply come from a pipe. Only a highly trained pastry chef could recreate these by hand, and no one could do it as quick. The classic Viennetta cake has twelve layers and takes six seconds to make. In 1981, Wall's ice cream concept developer Kevin Hillman conceived the idea for this ice cream cake. It was marketed as a Christmas speciality a year later. And it succeeded. In the Netherlands, one in ten people now eats Viennetta as a Christmas dessert. During the corona pandemic, Viennetta consumption increased significantly in a fit of anxiety-reducing nostalgia. Viennetta was withdrawn from the market in Indonesia until a petition signed by nearly 75,000 sweet-brick-craving people brought it back. Though Unilever now produces this ice cream dessert, it remains a popular product.

Have you ever been to a design museum?

You walk around and look at exceptional chairs, vases and lamps. Imagine carrying a bag of gummy bears with you and leaving one of the coloured ursine-like sweets on a pedestal. Just lick its bottom and stick it down. There you go. It has found its place. Though it may escape most people's attention, an exhaustive design process has preceded many food products. Yet you hardly ever come across food in a museum, except in its restaurant. The food design process is often more complex and elaborate than the design process of, to say, a vase or chair. So food also

breath taking !

on the left you can see the design collection of Barilla.

deserves a place in the museum! Almost all of the vegetables you buy nowadays have gone through years of seed cultivation. Most lettuces, especially in Northern Europe and America, have been cultivated so that a sweeter taste replaces most of their natural bitterness. The milky, bitter juice you see when you tear lettuce contains a morphine-like substance that the Romans used to aid sleep. Almost all supermarket fruit and vegetables are designed. As a result, they are sweeter, fit better in packaging, wilt less quickly, and look nicer. (See chapter Next Nature.)

After thirty years of crossbreeding, Bayer introduced an onion that doesn't make you cry when sliced. The onion is now the property of BASF. Given their five-million-dollar investment and years of research and development, you can imagine that they have high expectations for the 'tearless' onion. Who knows, maybe it will eventually dominate the market, just like the orange carrot. Another Bayer invention is tomatoes that are more firmly attached to the branch and thus require less packaging. Small tomatoes used to detach easily from the green truss. Packing them in a sealed plastic box kept them from rolling around your grocery bag. Then truss-holding tomatoes came along that only needed a cardboard box with a wrapper. These developments aim to please the consumer, whereas, in the past, the design work that went into producing vegetables was for the manufacturer's benefit. Other examples are crops with a higher yield and resistance to diseases. These cultivation processes can take up to thirty years, which makes investment decisions difficult. I know very few chairs or vases that are preceded by thirty years of development. Indeed, you may only see such design processes within architecture. If you find that comparison unfair because you think cultivating plants is very different from designing an object or building, then consider industrially produced food.

What, for example, does it take to manufacture a Magnum? You might think it's just 'normal' vanilla ice cream covered in chocolate. However, you can't freeze 'normal' chocolate to minus forty degrees Celsius. So the Magnum's production required more intelligence and innovation than you think!

Designing food for mass production requires considerable research and experimentation. Not only should it have a beautiful shape, but it also has to be tasty. Otherwise, it won't sell. 'Tasty' is not enough, by the way. It has to be the perfect combination of sweet, salty and fat so that the brain experiences a small but explosive culinary orgasm when you take a bite. After which, you immediately want to take another bite. The product must also have a long shelf life and be safe, hygienic and stable. As well as taste, there is also consistency and mouthfeel to consider. Even the 'bite sound' can influence the final design: food should, above all, sound 'fresh'. At the same time, it must also fit into a production process and not stick to the assembly line, for example, or fall apart after a few days. The colour must not fade too quickly, and it should smell nice and stay that way. The raw materials must be readily available and consistent in quality. And all this should not be too expensive, because industrial food is high design but low culture. Finally, in addition to all the product developments, the packaging is also of critical importance. It must be appropriate, appeal to the consumer, be able to compete on price, meet expectations, and fit into the cultural context. Selling milk in a plant sprayer may be original, but not commercial.

Industrial food is so fascinating in terms of design and technology that it deserves its own museum. But wait, this museum already exists! We don't know it as a museum. It's called a supermarket. Here, we can see an exhibition of industrial food every day of the week, and it's free to get in!

Walk around the supermarket like a surprised gnome (see chapter Afrocado), and you feel like Alice in Wonderland visiting Charlie and the chocolate factory. You discover there are oat cows, chickens that lay chocolate eggs and vegetarian pigs. You see fish in cuboid form for the first time: how do they swim in the sea? Now, you can hardly call fish fingers 'complex' in terms of design. Instead, they are 'minimal' or 'absurd'. Today, these fish sticks – which in no way resemble fish and no one asked for – are eaten extensively worldwide. But this didn't happen by itself. Paul Josephson (he calls himself Mr Fish Stick and hates fish fingers) wrote the fascinating history of the fish finger in his research paper 'The Ocean's Hot Dog'. This product was introduced in America in 1953, just as most people were first acquiring freezers. Americans were fervent fish-haters at the time because of its rapid decay and the effort it took to bring fish from the ocean inland and keep it fresh. However, the Second World War and the development of more powerful engines and better equipment led to a fish surplus. The fish was frozen in large blocks on board the fishing vessels to prevent decay. Fish producers would offer the blocks for housewives to cut off 'made to measure' pieces. But with filets sticking together, it became a mess. Then they came up with a shape that Americans were familiar with: the sausage or hot dog. The result was a small, elongated stick with rounded corners.

A shape was devised for the 'fish-hating' Americans that matched something they were already familiar with: the hot dog.

The technology developed then is still used today. The fish blocks went through an X-ray machine to scan for bones and then were sawn into smaller pieces. The product was now more suited to the consumer but was far from a hit. The breakthrough came when marketer Paul Jacobs of Gordon's Fish Fingers from Massachusetts launched a major advertising campaign aimed at the busy housewife. She received a brief respite from her demanding daily routine by serving easy-to-prepare fish fingers. Jacobs placed large advertisements in influential magazines, calling fish fingers 'the industry's greatest contribution to modern living.' His innovation seamlessly aligned with the post-war modernism of the 1950s. Slowly, there was a shift in the market and magazines published recipes such as 'fish fingers with spaghetti'. A large government subsidy for the fishing sector followed a year after the fish finger's launch, giving promotion and sales an extra boost. When the School Lunch Program was launched in the late 1940s, Gordon's Fish Fingers lobbied vigorously for years to get fish fingers on the menu. They succeeded, and because children now grew up with them, the (essentially very neutral tasting) fish finger was fully embraced and passed down through the generations. Like the Viennetta, fish finger consumption also rose during the pandemic. Some countries even saw fish finger consumption rise by over fifty per cent. Brandi McKuin, a researcher at the University of California, Santa Cruz, researched frozen fish products. Surprisingly, she found that fish fingers are quite sustainable, with a climate impact almost equal to tofu.

Austrian architect duo Martin Hablesreiter and Sonja Stummerer (Honey and Bunny) made an iconic photo. They cut a rectangle out of a fish and inserted a snug-fitting fish finger into it. The image is part of their book and documentary Food Design, in which they analytically and visually discuss mass production in the food industry. They show that the shape of food is created in different ways because, for example, it has to fit into a machine or a child's hand. Or the form should feel nice in your mouth, like Pringles. They explain how expectations and cultural context play a role in this. You slice a round loaf of bread and cut a round cake or a pizza into slices, but you don't cut a round hamburger. Mouthfeel and texture are also culturally determined. The 'hardness' of chocolate differs per country. In Asia, slimy foods such as okra, natto and slimy desserts have a culinary position, whereas many in the west consider slimy foods gross. Martin and Sonja's research also shows how industry can make complex products in large numbers. For example, products with a liquid core and crispy casing, such as chocolates with liqueur on the inside and a crunchy layer of almond flakes on the outside. But it's not only chocolate that can be filled with liquid. Tiny fat globules in low-fat milk can also be 'inflated' with water by means of a sieve.

This process allows you to consume lean, but you taste fat. Their book and documentary teach you why sugar cubes are square, Pringles are stackable, and fish fingers are rectangular (it makes them useful for production, transport and packaging). The round shape of bread and cake is inconvenient, but square shapes are undesirable for reasons of nostalgia. We like the idea of eating an artisanal product, even if it is industrially made.

Martin and Sonja brilliantly show you things that are right under your nose that you have probably paid little attention to. Martin tells me they are interested in everyday, almost invisible things. 'We have thousands of things around us that we don't think of as "designed", but they are. These things affect us in some way. Sometimes they are literally part of us. In a sense, all these edible and inedible things around us determine our habits: how we think and what we consider normal. What surprises and saddens us is that people are very interested in phones, cars and other machines but know little about their food. This is why we make our work.' Their next book was Eat Design, which was not about the food itself, but about how we deal with it. It includes a flood of images. A cappuccino with a slice of salami on the rim like a lime slice in a cocktail. A shelf at IKEA full of crockery and food on top. Sonja eats in an IKEA showroom at a table with a price tag on it. They sit in restaurants with swimwear (diving goggles and swimming cap), eating while wearing construction helmets or completely naked. Sonja, dressed in evening attire, is about to split a turban cake with a chainsaw. Martin dips a frankfurter into his jacket's mustard-filled breast pocket. Each image makes you wonder what is not right and why it is not right. By showing what is strange and making you feel likewise, you discover how rigid and limited our eating standards are. (See chapter Crooked.) What Martin and Sonja do is pure. They reflect our dealings with food without judgment and with heaps of imagination. They disarm and open your gaze to show that a whole world can lie behind the simplest of things.

Hardly anyone who buys a tube of Pringles realises these are officially biscuits and not potato chips in England. They are made from a dough of potato, corn starch and rice, which reduces the tax liability of the company that makes them. We particularly look down on mass-produced foods. And yes, ultra-processed foods contain few to no unprocessed ingredients. They are cheap and often unhealthy. But they are there. The moment you decide to be 'against' the industry, you also decide that you don't want to see its beauty. Our prejudices stand in the way of a fresh look that recognises things are not so black and white. Many people depend daily on these products, and by no means is every industrialised product bad. Industrialisation also allows more people to eat on a smaller budget. What if we use industrialisation for quality and health?

This might seem tantamount to blasphemy. However, it's worth remembering that one of the principles of the Bauhaus (the renowned German school of art and design from the 1920s) is that well-designed products are affordable and accessible to all. You can even see the geometric shapes of the food industry as derived from the Bauhaus style. Place a Toblerone, Oreo and KitKat so that the Toblerone is on the left and diagonally above the KitKat. Place the Oreo above the top right corner of the KitKat. And there you have it: an edible Bauhaus composition. It could go straight into the museum. Or wait, let's go to the museum right now!

challenge

visit the Food Design Museum (a.k.a. the supermarket)

Scan the QR code you'll find here: **www.marijevogelzang.nl/lickit** and take your phone and headphones to the supermarket. Take a real museum tour there!

phone eats first

Food styling is the Paris Hilton of working with food: it's nice to see but also a bit meaningless. Most people assume that because I'm a designer who works with food, I'm a food stylist and fill my days decorating and photographing plates of food while humming the Sound of Music. This is not the case.

If you look at my website, you will see that I make sure my work looks attractive. Then why am I not a stylist? That's because I see my work's aesthetic as the language with which I want to communicate. First, I think about what I want to say. Such as tap water is extraordinary, food can act as a binding agent between people from different backgrounds, or you can activate memories memories of the Second World War with certain smells and tastes. Only when I know what I want to communicate, do I make aesthetic choices that support this. The aesthetic value is hence a 'by-product' of what I make. Styling is, as it were, the language with which I communicate my message. I never make anything just for its beauty.

Without a message, a beautiful shape is nothing more than an empty shell.

An aesthetic, or 'form language' is also a language. Screaming louder doesn't necessarily make people listen better. As with spoken or written language, it matters how you communicate with visual language. I want to ensure that what I make will reach or touch the viewer consciously or unconsciously. I want people to see what I am trying to say so that they become attentive to it and enthusiastic and want to listen. But if you don't know what you want to say, it doesn't do you much good. This applies to all forms of language. You can formulate nice words – like campaigning politicians seeking election – but they are often hollow phrases. Without a message, a beautiful shape is nothing more than an empty shell. But if you know what you want to say, it is easier to find the appropriate formal language. I am certainly not arguing against visual art: I enjoy an exciting composition, strong use of colour and beautifully weighted lines. Such qualities help convey an image's power of expression. Although the image does not use words per se, it can still speak to you. Though poetry might not convey logic, it has the power of expression.

Language comes out of your mouth, and food goes in.
'Aesthetic' comes from the Greek verb aisthánomai and means something like 'to perceive'. You probably associate perception with 'to look', but you do that with your eyes, whereas you perceive with all your senses. Anyone who eats Toblerone knows you can also perceive its shape with your mouth. The visual aspect of food is essential and sometimes seems to overshadow its taste. Who still feels a mango or smells a pineapple to see if it's ripe? Who knocks on a watermelon to hear if it is good (the hollower, the better, a Turkish stall holder taught me at the market). You mainly see pre-packaged food at the supermarket. And anyone who gets too frisky with the fruit and veg runs the risk of being considered a pervert. So in the Netherlands, you see mangoes and avocados in packaging that says 'ripe to eat' (eetrijp) so that your eyes read what you could have used your other sense for. You only judge the food with your eyes. At home when I was a child, I used to get an unattractive blob on my plate and had to be content with it. It didn't have to look pretty. It didn't have to be on Instagram.

I once heard someone in China say, 'The phone eats first.' Take a picture first, then eat. Our eyes often taste the food before our nose even gets a whiff. We visually scan food with our eyes, looking for clues about how it will taste. Our previous eating experiences lead us to expect a red strawberry will be sweet. We construct a taste profile in our heads. This also explains the success of cooking programmes because people can 'taste' along at home. Although we use all our senses in the background, our eyes dominate. Sight is our alpha sense. And therein lies the problem because when our eyes create taste expectations based on what we already know, they never really 'taste' anything new.

The exhibition 'Feast for the Eyes' was, as the title suggests, a show with beautiful photographs of food. It was a spectacular selection of photographic images about the history of food presented at the C/O Berlin exhibition space for photography. They asked me to make a performance that echoed the exhibition's theme. The exhibition ensured the eyes, in particular, were well 'nourished'. In response, I made a 'Food Massage Salon' that activated all the senses except the eyes because the exhibition catered for them plentifully. Giant hammocks hung in the exhibition space. Visitors who wanted a treatment at the 'salon' could get into the hammock and were blindfolded by a 'food massage therapist'. The blindfold had a hole in it for the nose and mouth, making you look like a life-sized banana with a face. As you lay in the gently swaying hammock, blindfolded and wearing a pair of headphones, your body received a massage while you heard a voice: the voice of your tongue! It starts out shy but grows slightly angry:

'Normally, I'm always quiet. But, I have to say, I'm kind of mad at you. You've been so focused on your eyes lately that I feel ignored. You seem to be ignoring your whole body. You act like you're nothing more than eyes on legs. You look at a computer screen, a telephone and other people. You touch a screen more often than another human being. And when you eat, you eat in a hurry or in front of your laptop, and you don't properly taste what you eat. How did it come to this? In the old days, you put everything in your mouth and touched everything. I remember your first bite of sand and that time you put a cable in your mouth. I know what dust and hair taste like and how Lego bricks feel in your mouth. You may not remember the taste of an ice cream mixed with your snot bubble, but I do. I was there when you fell and tasted the metallic flavour of blood. I've been with you all this time. I know what your first real kiss was like. How sweet and clumsy you were!'

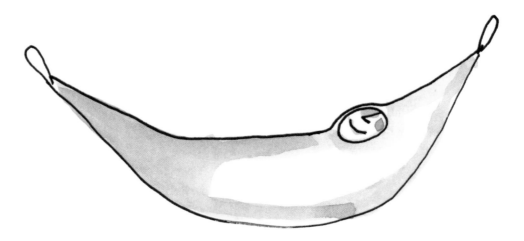

Could you perhaps give your tongue a little more and your eyes a little less?

'But step by step, you started to use me less. I know you hate it when you try to pronounce a word in a foreign language and I can't turn in the right direction so quickly. And I know you bite me now and then when you are tense. It hurts. Still, it's nice to be your tongue. I think we can have many more adventures, taste flavours, experience textures and discover the world.'

While you listen to your slightly angry but above all sweet tongue, the therapist gives you a 'treatment'. You feel a soft, lickable sugar and coconut butter scrub on your lips. You get a compact mask of nourishing yoghurt spread on your face and fed into your mouth. A brush dipped in rum caresses your tongue. You feel the chill of ice while smelling a mist of orange blossom water. Then you get a little tahini (gooey sesame paste) squirted into your mouth, right between your lower lip and bottom teeth. You get a spoonful of finely cut, crunchy apple cubes while listening to a beat through the headphones. By chewing, you make an 'inner head' concert with the sound of the apple cubes. The nine different eating experiences ultimately lead you to your tongue's all-important question: could you perhaps give your tongue a little more and your eyes a little less? This is not simply what your tongue wants; it knows it is also good for you. You were born with all your senses, and your tongue knows you are much happier when you use all of them.

Though this unique massage parlour is about the senses other than the eyes, I still ensure that everything looks attractive. The therapists wear clean white shirts with a light-yellow glow-in-the-dark logo. White porcelain objects specially made for this experience sit on white trolleys. The room conveys the atmosphere of a professional beauty salon, except for its location: the middle of the museum, among the photos on the wall. Why did I go to all this trouble if you're going to be blindfolded, and the whole point is to pay less attention to the eyes? It is because I want to seduce you with the formal language. The aesthetic speaks to you and makes you want to lie down in the unusual hammock to indulge in an unfamiliar but aesthetically pleasing experience. I know it's a little intimidating. That is why the overall appearance is imperative. The clean, attractive, familiar and safe environment is made with care. I often work with white textiles for their reference to white linen restaurant tablecloths and a chef's toque blanche. White allows you to see at a glance whether everything is clean. So if you step into a strange situation and surrender yourself blindfolded to a stranger, there is comfort in knowing hygiene has been observed. White also exudes a particular serenity that feeds into the story I want to tell. My choice of white textiles speaks of careful attention to detail. The styling serves the purpose and feeling I want to achieve. In this context, I am refashioning the famous statement 'form follows function' to 'form follows feeling'.

Since the ancient Greeks, we have referred to the eyes and ears as 'higher senses'. (See chapter Smell.) Our other senses increasingly fade into the background. We stand with one virtual foot in the metaverse, where our eyes are in command. Meanwhile, the other foot wants to walk in a natural forest where we can smell the resin and moss, the wind strokes our cheeks, and we can listen to twigs snapping under our feet. We can go there when our work at a desk behind a computer – where time, seasons and our life cycle no longer seem to matter – is done. Because of this, food's role as a conduit to life's sensory pleasures is growing. You smell, taste, hear, see and touch something you put into your body. It's not just anything you're consuming. They are not Lego blocks. It grew, as a plant, for example, and can now be part of you. Let your eyes rest for a moment. Close them, and surrender to all your other senses.

What happens when you close your eyes?
What do you give space and attention to without your sight?

Suppose I want to feed you. We do not know each other. I'm standing before you, holding a spoon of strawberries and whipped cream. Strawberries: delicious. And yet you probably feel a little uncomfortable as I am standing in front of you with a spoon, ready to put in your mouth. We probably look at each other politely, feeling uncomfortable with our awkward and socially correct smiles. You would graciously and slightly uncomfortably open your mouth. At that point, I would shove the strawberries into your mouth, equally gracious and uncomfortable, and try not to get too much whipped cream on your upper lip. You chew but don't properly taste the strawberries, so you can't tell whether they are flavoursome. It would be easier if we got to know each other first. But even then, it would feel strange. Because how often does someone feed you now that you're an adult?

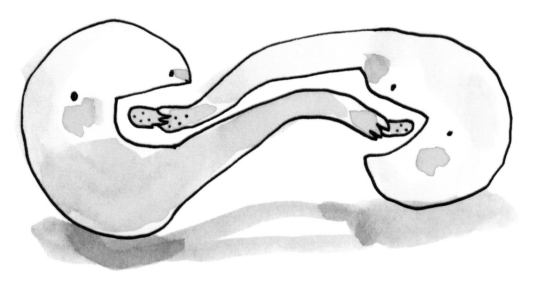

For years I sought an answer to the question: can I make strangers feed each other without discomfort? A personal experience triggered this question. When I, having just given birth, breastfed my newborn son from the maternity bed, my mother started to feed me. She fed me, and I fed my son. I thought the way history was repeating itself here was remarkable. At the same time, I had a slightly uneasy feeling. Feeding is a wellspring of our human connection, but we sometimes get disconnected. Feeding each other is something intimate. Something that we associate with surrender and the emotional balance of power. Yet it is a universal human activity. Every human was once a baby who was fed. However, it's something you hardly ever experience as a healthy adult. Maybe your loved one feeds you snacks at a restaurant. Your child might feed you snacks as a game. But suppose I were to feed you. We make no eye contact. You breathe in and out slowly. I feed you. You taste. You listen when I talk. You can relax.

Feeding someone feels uncomfortable. A blindfold or tablecloth takes away that discomfort.

I used to give workshops in Copenhagen, Saint Petersburg and Tokyo, analysing the effects and actions of feeding people under different conditions. What happens when you feed people to the beat of a big drum or while they are listening to someone tell a story? What if you hold hands? What if you feed them without eye contact? I discovered that every place has cultural differences, but the principle of feeding is universal. It creates intimacy. I saw strangers brushing off each other's mouths and guiding hands to take a sip of water in between.

Taking away eye contact made a big difference. You can remove a lot of discomfort by wearing a blindfold or having a tablecloth over you. In Budapest, I made an installation with Roma women, a marginalised group in Hungary. Ten women fed as many as four hundred visitors in four days. They told their life stories based on the simple dishes they had the audience taste. The guest sat under a table with a long white tablecloth over it. The guest could hear one of the women and taste her food but not see her. The tablecloth prevented eye contact. The situation created a strange anonymity, and the guest visibly relaxed. They not only tasted but also listened and sympathised; there was room for emotion and connection. The food was simple: bread with lard, green peppers, and oranges. It wasn't about food, but this experience was impossible without food. It wasn't about the eyes either, but the same experience would not have been possible with full vision. It makes you wonder what else our eyes are hiding from us. What do we observe if we close them for a while?

challenge

taste with your mouth and your ears!

You may have heard of Dining in the Dark. I once went to a version in Berlin (which is amusingly called UnsichtBar). I found it particularly special to be served by people who are blind and who navigated effortlessly through the dark space while the guests required assistance. It probably also boosted my melatonin production because I became incredibly sleepy. Yet the experience of visual uncertainty is exciting in regard to food. What effect does temporarily removing your vision have on your sense of taste?

Now you can eat at home in the dark (you should try it at least once), but what if you shift your attention from your eyes to your ears? Go to **www.marijevogelzang.nl/lickit** and download the audio file linked to this chapter. Here's what you do.

- Pour a large glass of fresh water.
- Listen to the audio through headphones.
- You will now hear several different sounds.
- Concentrate, close your eyes, and take a sip of water with every sound.
- Allow the water to pass through your mouth for a moment before swallowing.
- Note below the subtle differences in taste you perceive with each sound and sip.

sip I

sip 2

sip 3

sip 4

sip 5

sip 6

sip 7

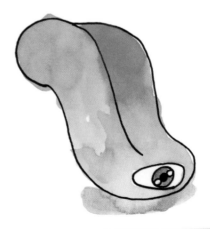

so, that's
$ 10,- for you.
I'll withhold it
from your
pocket money

free

Leon Barre is among the last graduates of Food Non Food, my department at the Design Academy Eindhoven. He is one of the department's most engaging students, always full of energy, ready to help others and regularly initiating extra activities. On graduation day, Leon stands in front of us with a dishevelled fringe and wearing a striped shirt. He holds up a sign that reads: 'Etymology of the word "free". Old English: freo. From Indo-European root, meaning to love.' He added that the word 'gratis' comes from 'graceful'.

Leon hands out free soup. A simple act of love and kindness. And though simple, his action is ingrained in a belief that small gestures make a difference in a world where anonymity and cold commerce prevail. Leon wondered, 'Why do we designers want to make things for the world if that world, first of all, needs a little more kindness?' He propounds this infectious notion from a charming mobile soup station. His project is modest and accommodating. It isn't a large soup kitchen for people who lack money. Ultimately, it is not about the soup: the soup is a medium. What matters is giving a good feeling. For the recipients, it feels as if they are receiving a personal gift. Leon's initiative is an example of a 'protopia', a small and realistic opposite of a dystopia. He serves several soups, one of which he dedicates to Charlie Chaplin for his fiery speech in the 1940 film 'The Great Dictator', in which he calls for countering intolerance, racism and aggression with kindness, cheerfulness and benevolence. He dedicates another to Benjamin Franklin for his generosity in favour of good. Franklin once loaned a friend money and insisted he did not have to pay him back. He would rather he lend it to someone else who could put it to good use and that person to the next person. The term 'pay it forward' arose from this. Leon makes his free soups with leftover market produce. He also 'grows his soup' in a communal garden.

What is the value of a free product for the recipient?

The soup must be free. The recipient does not have to pay, regardless of who they are or their wealth. I wonder whether Leon's initiative is sustainable, especially if he ends up homeless because of the free soup. After all, he has to pay his rent. A solution for this does not have to be at the expense of providing free soup. His project can also be sponsored. I also wonder: if something is free, what is its value to whoever receives it?

There's something odd about free.
Everyone likes free. If something is free, hardly anyone questions its usefulness – they'll just take it. People will risk the free thing disappointing them because not taking it would entail a much heavier sense of regret. And because it's free, you can dispose of it with the same ease. At conferences, I occasionally run into Dan Ariely, professor of Psychology and Behavioural Studies at Duke University. I love his research projects. There is something very disarming about them. While we were having breakfast in Puebla, Mexico, he once told me, 'People may think they are very rational, but they are not. They are very irrational.' All sorts of things influence our objective mind. Although we behave irrationally, our behaviour is predictable. Apparently, we almost always make the same illogical choices. So we are 'predictably irrational', which happens to be the title of Dan's book. We are often irrational, especially when it comes to food and money. Dan also did much research into the principle of freeness. 'Most transactions have an advantage and a disadvantage. But when something is free, we forget about the downsides. The free aspect gives us such an emotional boost that we start to think what is offered to us is much more valuable than it is. People appear to act as if something that is free costs less and yields a lot more than it actually does.'

A free product is at its most attractive just before you receive it.

Dan explains this human tendency with the help of a study from his book. He offered 398 students chocolates and monitored their reactions. He used cheap Hershey's Kisses and more expensive Lindt chocolates, which were clearly more luxurious and valuable. If the students could choose between a free Hershey's Kisses and a significantly discounted Lindt chocolate, they still preferred the free Hershey Kisses despite this not being the best deal objectively. The discount on the Lindt chocolates was more than the Hershey's chocolates cost. Even if something only costs a few cents, you will ask: do I want this, and am I willing to pay this amount? But if something is free, it's a no-brainer. 'Yes! Bring it on!' So a free product becomes very attractive just before you get it. And guess what? The expectation of a pleasurable experience, such as receiving something, releases more dopamine in the brain than the pleasurable experience itself. Moreover, a free product can then become worthless once you own it. If you don't invest in something, you are not invested in it.

A long time ago, as an impressionable rookie designer who was foregrounding food, I was asked to give a lecture at the Woonbeurs, a interior design trade fair in Amsterdam. Unfortunately, there was no budget. The lovely lady who invited me said it would be perfect for my 'exposure'. I went there, shoes polished, but I had to arrange a babysitter, for which, of course, I paid. I tried to entice her with the prospect of exposure, but funnily enough, that doesn't work for babysitters. Once at the location, only the lovely lady knew about my arrival. She was busy and quickly pointed me to an inflatable tent for lectures. The tent was an acoustic magnet which accumulated all of the trade fair's hubbub. I asked if my presentation had been announced, but the lovely lady wasn't sure because communication was not her department. She only procured the speakers. Fortunately, I met some friends at the fair who, just before the start, persuaded three more people to come and sit in the inflatable tent. I kept to my story as best I could in front of an audience of six very nice, enthusiastic people.

When people pay, they pay attention.

Had the organisation paid for my lecture – at least the fifty euros for a babysitter – they probably would have done a better job promoting the presentation. They probably would have said: 'Hey, I see part of the budget is being invested in this speaker. We have to ensure we communicate the presentation to the attendees. Otherwise, it's money wasted.' They would ensure their investment was not in vain. Afterwards, I heard people would have liked to attend my lecture at the fair but did not know it was taking place. If theatre tickets are free and all you have to do is reserve them, fewer people attend. As my mentor says, 'When people pay, they pay attention.'

How does this relate to Leon's soup?

It may be free, but it's not worthless. When free soup is given out at the supermarket, you may want it, but it often doesn't feel valuable. Leon's homemade soup, fresh from his soup station and served in amusing clay bowls, feels like a gift even if the soup is the same as in the supermarket. What if Leon asked for fifty cents for his soup so people would invest in it anyway? Funnily enough, and you probably already sensed this, in this case, the soup's value becomes less than when it is free. Once the soup has a price attached to it, it sprouts legs and steps from one world to the other. According to Dan, this is because we live in two different worlds when it comes to money: the market world and the social world. Both of these worlds have different norms. If you confuse the two, then things get complicated. Dan explains: 'Imagine you are visiting your in-laws on an important public holiday and have just eaten a delicious meal. Your mother-in-law has spent days preparing the most amazing food. Everyone is clearly enjoying it. You eat and drink and are appreciative of the conviviality. When dinner is over, you look at your mother-in-law gratefully and say, "Everyone enjoyed this delicious dinner. How much do you want for it?" You get up, grab your wallet and pull out some money. "Do you want two hundred? Three hundred?" What would happen? Why does it become awkward when money comes into play, yet you comfortably pay and tip in a restaurant? If you confuse the market and social norms, it's a mess. You can no longer count on an invitation from your mother-in-law. And you will surely be barred from any restaurant where instead of paying, you hug the chef and whisper in his ear the promise of exposure.'

In the past, money and food were one and the same. You would eat some apples from your tree and trade some for eggs. Roman Empire soldiers were given salt ('sale' in Italian) as 'salary'. Salt was also traded for a long time in China and East Africa. Bread, grain, turmeric, rum and cocoa have all been used as payment in various parts of the world. Even today, Parmesan cheese is sometimes used as collateral for a loan in Italy. Food can decay, so it is inconvenient to suddenly have a lot of fish if you want to exchange your catch for a pair of shoes. Money was created to replace goods and food symbolically. We no longer work for apples and eggs but money.

Money, it seems, has also taken the literal place of goods. If you think about it for a moment, it is not the money we crave but the freedom it offers, the security it promises, and the significance it bestows. Nowadays, we associate these qualities with money. But if we desire freedom, security and significance, shouldn't we focus on them directly and not by proxy? These are qualities independent of the amount in your bank account. As with food, money is only money if someone uses it as such. Otherwise, it is merely quantities of metal, pieces of paper or streams of zeros and ones.

Having money as an infallible substitute for food has created a schism in how we think about food. And about money. Since food no longer equates to money, many prefer cash over food. We eat notes and poop coins – as long as we can meet our basic needs. We conceived the money system to support and make our lives easier, but sometimes it seems that the roles have been reversed, with human lives now supporting the money system. And not only in people's lives but also in the food industry. I once did an art project with a poultry breeding company.

The farmer in question, Twan Engelen, doubted the ethics of keeping so many animals per square metre. I thought it was an extraordinary line of enquiry for someone who owned hundreds of thousands of chickens in closed sheds in De Peel and wanted to work with him. I wasn't interested in answering his question. My personal opinion didn't matter. I decided to let curiosity guide me.
(See chapter Afrocado.)

There are many discussions about broiler chickens and factory farming. The industrial chicken is still the world's most eaten animal, but most people have never seen a living broiler chicken. Chances are you've never heard of a breeding company either. That's because a breeding company does things you, the consumer, might not consider. It increases the number of chickens, like a sex farm for poultry. Hens outnumber roosters at this breeding company by ten to one. These are the parents of the broiler chickens we eat. The parents live about a year longer than their offspring. The hens' fertilised eggs are incubated at hatcheries, after which the chicks are fattened and slaughtered.

A chicken is a highly productive animal. Imagine you have one rooster and ten hens: Michael along with Joanne, Linda, Maria, Lisette, Conny, Yoko, Pauline, Geraldine, Iris and Bertie. This coterie can multiply in four generations (less than two years) to forty-six million chickens! That's sixty-five million tons of meat, a quarter of the Netherlands' annual chicken consumption.

Jesus's handing out of fish and loaves might impress you, but the everyday chicken is indeed a miracle to behold. For a good reason, Bill Gates uses chickens to fight poverty in developing countries. Chickens can be reproduced for meat, but they also lay eggs. Bill Gates' chickens are developed in the Netherlands and genetically bred so that, despite poor feed, inadequate shelter or a challenging climate, they continue to lay well and produce good meat. A production chicken is high design. If only the poor chickens were like pandas, they hardly have sex.

There is a potential chick in every egg.

Twan walked me through his company. You can't just come in. You must shower first to minimise the risk of infections because Twan doesn't want to use antibiotics for his animals. Because of this barrier, local residents often think mysterious things are happening and that Twan is a kind of Gargamel in a black dress, making Smurf ice cream according to a secret recipe. That's a pity because you can see Twan cares about his animals. Like the shrimp breeder (see chapter Shrimp Sex), he does his utmost to give the animals the best possible life. That is, of course, also good for production. The hens lay their fertilised eggs onto conveyor belts, after which they are gently collected. After a wash, they end up in high piles of cardboard trays. I see endless rows of eggs, each with a potential chick. It's like holding acorns in your palm, whereby some have the potential to become an oak tree one day.

A fertilised egg that has not yet been incubated does not yet contain a chick. The egg has only one fertilised cell. The chick grows when the chicken starts to brood. So you can just eat the egg. A hen lays several eggs in a few days and does not sit on the eggs until the cessation of laying, causing them to grow all at once.

I start thinking about money.

Because whoever has a rooster and some hens has capital. Of course, the chickens also have to eat and do not grow without some support. But they can consume what we don't eat. I clutch a fertilised egg in one hand and a euro in the other. The euro holds the promise of a transaction, but I can't eat it. I can eat the egg in all kinds of ways: boiled, as an omelette or raw. If I don't eat the egg, a chick may hatch. The chick will grow and start laying eggs that I can eat or, if a rooster is at hand, can breed new chicks. I can also produce meat that I can eat. I don't want to advocate eating animals here. Nevertheless, the process behind it is impressive. Most people the world over take eating chicken for granted. The low price of an entire factory farm chicken in the supermarket is astonishing, especially considering the demands of raising such an animal: hatching, growing, keeping it healthy, slaughtering, cleaning, packaging, transporting and maintaining food safety. I look at the euro in my other hand. That euro has remained the same. Maybe I'll take it to the bank and get some interest. But that will be minimal compared to the interest a chicken yields.

The Eggchange was an exchange office for eggs and thoughts.

I wondered if I could apply my design background to expose Twan's question to a wider audience. What if there was a new kind of currency? I imagined a currency of fertilised eggs. Not that I envision carrying fertilised eggs in a purse or wallet, but a lyrical vision can help you see the value of things you take for granted. I created a pop-up bank where you received your starting capital upon opening an account: one fertilised egg. You could eat the egg immediately, spending your 'money' as it were. You could also hatch it and grow your capital into a chicken and later into more eggs, more chickens, or more meat. I called the pop-up bank the 'Eggchange' because it was a kind of exchange office. People could exchange ideas about poultry farming, the economy and food. Twan could thus pose his question concerning the ethics of his occupation to a larger audience. Anyone who became a bank member, such as Queen Máxima of the Netherlands, a leading advocate of universal access to safe and ethical financial services, received a fertilised egg. Many people hatched their eggs and soon noticed a broiler chicken is different from a 'normal' chicken. By hatching, growing and ultimately slaughtering your chicken (see chapter Death), you learn more about chickens and yourself by doing rather than theory.

These chickens are designed to yield more meat.

When I hatched many broilers and raised them at my studio, I learned they have few feathers. This is because they live in crowded conditions in large sheds and do not necessarily need feathers for warmth. Due to their specific 'design', these chickens sacrifice lush plumage and use their energy to grow in a way that yields more meat. I always think the same about bald men. They also say they put their energy into other important things, right? Having little feathers also streamlines their slaughter (the chickens, not the men) because less plucking is involved. Another notable quality I noticed in these chickens is that they are very tame and gentle because aggressive tendencies are counterproductive in their usual crowded conditions. Don't let them jump from your hands to the ground, because they can't and will have a hard landing. Their knee joints also seem different from other chickens. Finally, I learned that people consider it very strange if you keep many broiler chickens in an attic. When I asked grandma if she wanted a nice chicken, she looked disconcerted and said, 'No! Those are pumped-up chickens, right? They're full of antibiotics!' I laughed and replied, 'Well, I didn't give them any.' Apparently, 'free' didn't carry much weight here.

challenge

what is your food worth?

Until the 1970s, it was customary for manufacturers in the Netherlands to set their goods' selling price. Sometimes they printed the price on the packaging, and the shops selling the products had to accept this. This allowed manufacturers to ensure a fair margin. Today, the supermarkets have the power to control prices, or rather the purchasing organisations behind the supermarkets. There are usually a handful of such organisations in each country. The Netherlands has five. They sit at the neck of the hourglass, between thousands of producers and manufacturers on one side and a few thousand supermarkets and millions of consumers on the other. These five organisations determine what is sold, what is produced and what the prices are.

You can buy a head of lettuce at the shop for less than one euro. That's a good deal. I don't think you could grow it for that amount. You probably pay attention to the price when you shop, but when you serve your family or friends food, you don't calculate the portion price. Food has moved from the world of market norms to the world of social norms.

Invite friends or family for this challenge.
Ask everyone to bring a homemade dish and cash. Think about how much your food should cost per serving. You can calculate the food costs, the energy cost and the cost of the time you have put into cooking your dish. Or you can come up with an intuitive price. No two chefs are the same, and something you've toiled over for three hours isn't necessarily better than something you put together in four minutes.

Put everything on the table, sit around it and sell your dishes to one another. If you feel like it, you can put price tags on them, but you can also keep shouting your price like market traders. You can barter, too! Add plenty of alcohol for a fascinating discussion. You have to pay for what you consume. Write down how much you pay for each dish on a napkin and calculate the total. Observe what happens when you superimpose market norms on top of social norms.

sitopia

'You can have a meeting while sitting around the kitchen table, preparing vegetables for soup: one person washes, another peels, and a third person uses a pestle and mortar. During the discussion, you work together toward a specific result. You can talk while looking at one another or concentrating on slicing the carrots. I think both activities – working with your head and your hands – are controlled by different circuits in your body. You can maintain a conversation while you work with your hands. Your hands work almost automatically while you talk. Many hands make light work, and the meeting becomes a joint project instead of time spent on the dry exchange of words. And if the meeting is disappointing, at least you'll have some good food at the end!'

I'm speaking with Tristram Stuart. It's an old-fashioned phone conversation, not a video call. 'I'll put you in my pocket and go to the vegetable garden,' he says. So there I was, in his trouser pocket while he sowed corn and talked to me through his earphones. You plant corn in clusters rather than rows because they are wind-pollinated like all other grasses. The proximity of clusters allows the wind to blow the pollen over the corn more effectively. Years ago, I read Tristram's book, 'Waste: Uncovering the Global Food Scandal', about the world's shocking food waste problem.

When Tristram started researching this issue in 2002, food waste was nowhere on the agenda. A lot has changed since then. 'There are hardly any companies now without food waste regulations,' he tells me. 'That doesn't mean we've eliminated wastage. Many good steps are being taken. We have seen a massive increase in initiatives that creatively use residual flows to make new and tasty things.' His Toast Ale project, for example, brews beer from fresh, unsold bread that would otherwise end up as waste.

Tristram lived for years on free food, food that would otherwise be thrown away.

In his book, Tristram recounts looking after some pigs when he was fifteen. Feeding the pigs was expensive, so he collected surplus food from a market and a school kitchen. Much of it was perfectly edible, and he realised we throw away huge amounts of good food. For years, Tristram lived on free food that would otherwise be thrown away. An expiration date says more about a manufacturer's liability than the food's edibility, safety and taste. The most ironic example is the best before date on salt. Himalayan salt is 250 million years old. But when packaged, it must have an expiry date. The sell-by dates on rice or other dried products are also nonsense. Tristram put food waste on the map worldwide. Food waste is absurd when you consider that hunger still affects hundreds of millions of people and continues to grow, especially since the pandemic and war in Ukraine.

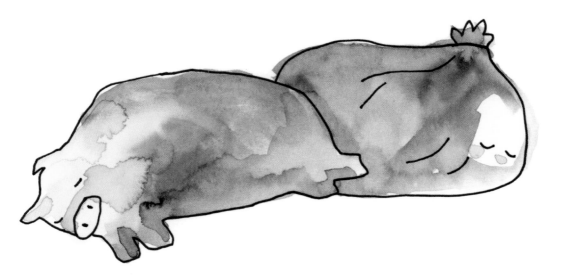

Alongside eliminating food waste and finding new uses for residual flows, Tristram wants a healthier world. 'The food system has the most significant negative impact on the world. It is the largest consumer of drinking water, contributes most to deforestation worldwide, and causes the most carbon dioxide emissions and mass extinction of plant and animal species. If the food system is the biggest disruptor in human relations with one another and with Earth, can we use that system to turn things around? Instead of depleting and eroding the soil, can we improve it by binding plant matter in the soil? (See chapter Good.) Can we use the food system to restore natural balance worldwide and bring people closer together and closer to their food?'

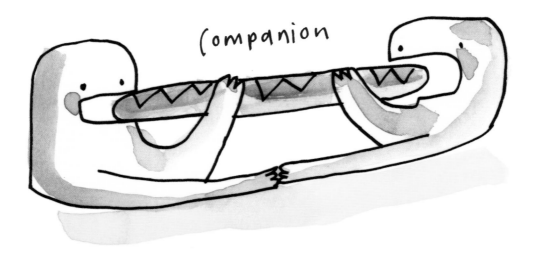

'Companionship is an important word for me,' Tristram says, assuring me that what I hear in the background is him filling a watering can. 'Companion comes from the Latin "panis", meaning bread. Originally, the word meant someone with who you share bread, a bread mate. Humans don't just share bread; we share a world with other organisms. We shall have to find a way of living together as friends. The notion of exchange – of trade – has always underpinned our society. Even though we used to trade using assets such as fish and wool, human exchange still binds us. We are dependent on one another through exchanges. We share bread with one another as a global community. Good companionship is the very foundation of our existence. Between people, but also between people, animals and the earth.' The war between Russia and Ukraine is a sad example of how disrupting companionship directly disrupts food distribution.

Tristram continues, 'I know there are always people that say, "That all sounds very nice and romantic, but what about the increasing world population? How are we going to feed ten billion mouths by 2050? We shall have to intensify our production methods even more because otherwise, we shall not be able to meet the demand." And that may be true if we continue consuming at the current rate. The fact is, we are already producing one and a half to two times more calories than we need.'

Disrupting companionship often means disrupting food distribution.

According to author Carolyn Steel, the United States produces five thousand calories per capita daily. This includes babies! An adult needs about two thousand calories. 'Many people eat much more than they need, but many also go hungry,' says Tristram. 'Those calories produced are also used to feed the animals we eat. Must we keep eating meat and dairy on a large scale? The great paradox is in the word "need".'

Ten billion people will soon need feeding.
But raise your hand: who needs Coca-Cola? It is an unnecessary type of nourishment. Tristram points out that we need a healthy planet and healthy food. 'We need a regenerative system. Otherwise, we'll be clinging to a sinking ship. What can you do in a practical sense? You can propose a levy on meat or carbon dioxide emissions, but nobody wants to pay more taxes. Let's use taxpayers' money, of which governments worldwide dedicate seven hundred billion dollars to agricultural subsidies already spent. Currently, one per cent of those subsidies go to ecological agriculture, and ninetynine per cent go to conventional agriculture – for junk food actually.'

'The word "company" also comes from the word "companion",' says Tristram. 'Together, you earn money and "share your bread". Exchange and trade are ingrained in people and society. The more companies aim to support the world, instead of eating nature and shitting money, the more likely we can leave a healthier world to our children. And that starts simply by teaching your children how things grow and by cooking and eating together.' Tristram says that he maintains his vegetable garden with a small community. 'It's about prioritising food. This priority can be as big or as small as you want.'

Look at the world through the lens of food.
Why don't we do this regularly? Television producer, fair-trade advocate, Tony's Chocolonely founder and novelist Teun van de Keuken explains this proposition more or less as follows. We might spend an entire afternoon and a lot of money choosing the perfect pair of jeans. But then we go to the supermarket and unthinkingly fill our trolley with junk. Why do we pay so little attention and respect to our food yet put that food in the body we squeeze into those expensive jeans?

Even in cultures where culinary traditions are deeply rooted, cheap and ultra-processed foods are steadily becoming part of the diet. I'm speaking with Carolyn Steel. She tells me this is because food is so vast and extensive that we simply don't see it. 'Everything is food,' she asserts. 'Food shapes our cities, landscapes, politics and society. Food shapes our bodies and economic system. Food influences social interactions, status and relationships between humans, animals, plants and raw materials. Food gives meaning to rituals. Food can connect, but it can also exclude. Food is power. Food is nature, culture, science and technology. Eating is the first thing we do when we come into this world, and it keeps us alive. Food is so profound, so all-encompassing and at the same time so mundane that we are not aware that food influences everything. It is us. We are made of food. Or, as Alan Watts describes it, try biting your own teeth, or try touching the tip of your index finger with the same index finger. You can't do it.'

Food flows have shaped our cities.

In her book, 'Hungry City', Carolyn, originally an architect, demonstrates how food has shaped our cities. In my city, there is the Fish Market, the Pig Market, a Sugar Street, a Wine Street and a Potato Market. Look in your hometown to see if there are streets named after food. Usually, these were places where the eponymous food entered or was traded. Food flows have shaped our cities. Waterways channelled boats with fresh produce from the surrounding areas, and the market was the city's heart. Food came from outside the city. Humans would eat the food, and the excretion they produced was collected and used as manure. Those on ocean-going vessels, and thus with access to the sea, were more likely to stave off the threat of hunger than those on river boats. With the arrival of the railway, fresh food came from further afield. Ultimately, a fine-mesh network of waterways, railways, motorways and airways was created, all connecting to the coronary artery and the heart: the city. Though the city no longer shapes its outskirts, distant and seemingly unrelated continents are coloured by what the city eats and excretes.

Never hungry again!
This promise was made in Europe after the Second World War. Farmers were expected to intensify their practices, specialise and increase production. It worked! Food became more affordable and more plentiful. Although food prices are rising again and more and more people rely on food banks, the proportion of income that people spend on food is still much lower than at the beginning of the twentieth century. The current food system has produced cheap food and fed many mouths. However, as Carolyn says sharply, 'Cheap food doesn't exist! You always pay the price somewhere, whether it is the loss of biodiversity, the depletion of agricultural land or the destruction of the seabed. We act as if nature were free, but it is not. Ultimately, we have to pay the price.'

Carolyn argues that the current food system will become a dystopia. For some, it already is. 'The extent to which we have lost our connection with food, nature and life means we now need a new vision. A vision that does not move toward food but flows from the food itself. Imagine how food moves to the periphery of people's lives. Now envisage a drawing in front of you and you standing in the middle of a circle. That circle is "life". You are in the centre, and the food is on the circle's periphery. You work and earn money to buy food. Now imagine food as a red dot in the centre. And you're on top of that dot. Food becomes the core, and from there, you start living. Would anything change? A paradigm shift can happen when you start seeing life through the lens of food. Food is the most powerful medium for making our lives and planet healthy because, as I already mentioned, it affects everything. By restoring our relationship with food, we can find better and more fulfilling ways to live because, ultimately, it's not about the food itself; it's about having a good life. And food can be our key to this.'

We live in a 'Sitopia', a world where food affects us on every level.

Carolyn does not propose to pursue a utopia but to make the best of the 'sitopia' in which we already live. The word is a compound of the Greek words 'sitos' and 'topos': food and place. Making the best of the sitopia we are in starts with realising we have a choice. We live in a world where food affects us on every level. As an example, imagine the following. Every Wednesday, you drink tea with your mother. It is your regular ritual. The tea is on sale, so you buy three packs. The tea you drink affects the life of a farmer in India. Hence, he can send his daughter to school. The farmer has to use pesticides for his tea, which impoverishes his soil. The bank only wants to give him a new loan for more land if he sells the tea to a large purchasing organisation. Forests are cut down for the new land. The large purchasing organisation packages the worst quality tea in bundles, adds flavouring, and sells it in Europe. The best quality is bought as an asset. The tea is transported by ship. The cargo ship is leaking oil and polluting the sea. Import duties must be paid. A trade agreement ensures that this tea can only be sold in Europe. Menopausal women often drink this tea because, according to an influencer, it is very healthy.

The moment we realise that food encompasses and affects everything, we acquire a superpower. According to Carolyn, this is when we can switch to the right kind of sitopia: one based on a good life. But, what is a good life? This will be different for everyone, but if you look at the number of diseases of affluence, burnout and depression, you notice a trend. There is a need for an alternative movement. The pandemic demonstrated the need for human proximity, for time and rest, for going to the office when you want to and not because you have to, and for time to eat and time to grow and make it yourself. A good life starts with good food. Eating well means it is healthy for your body, it is tasty, it makes you happy, and you feel connected with where it comes from or is going. You start a movement to transfer food from the periphery to the centre of your existence – the core – because you understand that everything is food.

This sitopia requires change. Most of the changes are mental and cultural, but it is also necessary, for example, that we start paying the actual price for food. 'So that cheap products become more expensive,' Carolyn says. She suggests using quality food as money or a medium of exchange. If you think Carolyn's sitopia is elitist, then think again. In a good sitopia, everyone can afford to eat well. What matters is that everyone has a good life, including the people who pick the hazelnuts in Turkey, the farmers and the fishers, but also the microbes in the soil, the primeval forests and the bees. A good life starts with pleasure, feeling part of something bigger, and feeling what you are doing matters.

A life without food is no life at all. We are made of food!

Carolyn shows us that food shapes the world. It's kind of a superpower – as if food stole Thanos's infinity gauntlet and rules the world. (That's why Thanos has a beard that looks like it was groomed with a rake. He is secretly a farmer!) Suppose you assume that food is only food when eaten. In that case, it is always connected with humans – those irrational, emotional, loving, longing, and connected human beings with a creative and narrative spirit. The complexity of food seems far removed from you, but when you see that it is you, that you are made of food, then you don't need to understand the complexity. Like not knowing how your brain works, but you can still think, or not knowing how your lungs work, but you can still breathe. A life without food is no life at all. But a life with food and without connection with others is not a life either. It's actually very straightforward. Share some bread with others and use your creative thinking skills. Ultimately, you decide with your imagination how you experience food, and life.

challenge

eat in good company

This challenge consists of several pages of invitations to eat with others. After all, it all starts with food and the connection you make with other people. You can tear out the page (a very old-fashioned thing to do) and send it to someone. You can also take a picture of the page and send it via instant messaging. Whatever you do, keep it relaxed; it doesn't have to be perfect. Most of all, have fun and share your dinner on instagram: @lickit.book.

Hello!
I'm having an invasive dinner, so I'm inviting myself to your place.

I shall arrive at your place on (date)   at
I shall bring foraged invasive species ingredients. It depends a bit on where I live, but it'll probably be Himalayan balsam, Japanese knotweed, crayfish or raccoon.

Make yourself something to eat, too, because I don't know whether I'll be able to rustle it all up. I shall bring a nice bottle of

Let me know if you'll let me in at the above time by responding to this invite via (phone number or email address)

Best regards,

invasive dinner

PS: I also wanted to tell you

Dear stranger,

Hello! You do not know me. I am
You might know me through this person or place

I should like to invite you to dinner.
I want to / don't want to* woo you! And / But* I want to do a challenge from the book **Lick It!**
And I like to meet new people. You can also bring someone with you.

I shall prepare a dish that tells something about me. Do you want to do the same?
Come to (place)
Date   time
RSVP to this invite via (telephone number or email address)

Best regards,

Hello Stranger

*Delete as appropriate

PS: I also wanted to tell you

Hi, I miss you!

I haven't seen you in so long and should like to cook something delicious for you.
Send me your favourite recipe, and I shall make it for you.
Will you come dressed as someone else so I can get to know you again?

Come to (place)
Date   time
RSVP to this invite via (telephone number or email address)

Best regards,

PS: I also wanted to tell you

Hey, I'm so sad.
Will you cheer me up?

I am sad because

I should like to receive comfort food, such as

If you visit, would you feed this to me too?
You don't need to add salt. I will cry into the food.

Come to (place)
Date   time
RSVP to this invite via (telephone number or email address)

Best regards,

will you come
and comfort me?

PS: I also wanted to tell you

Will you join me for a midnight picnic?

We shall have a midnight picnic at full moon.
Will you bring something round and white to eat?
Wear black clothes to avoid distractions in the dark.

We shall meet at (place)
Date   time
RSVP to this invite via (telephone number or email address)

Best regards,

will you join me at night?

I'm madly in love with you!

I'd love to kiss you and feed you aphrodisiac snacks using my mouth. (Which always seems like a lot of fun but could end up a bit gross.) Then we might have a wild night. But if you just want to sleep, that's also okay. I'll hold you in my arms, smell your hair, and pretend you're an egg I'm about to hatch.

Can you wear your pyjamas and have messy hair? I'll take care of the food.
Come to (place)
Date   time
RSVP to this invite via (telephone number or email address)

With tender kisses,

i'm pretty
In love
with you.

Hey, shall we take tasty treats to people in a nursing home?

Let's make food that's easy to chew.
For example

We can hand it out and also enjoy chatting with the people.

Come to (place)
Date   time
RSVP to this invite via (telephone number or email address)

Best regards,

PS: I also wanted to tell you

Hey neighbour!
You have won a free meal!

We don't speak often, but I see that you're busy sometimes.
I thought I'd cook an extra portion, especially for you!
I'll bring it by on
Date   time

Can you tell me if this works for you and if you have any dietary requirements?
RSVP to this invite via (telephone number or email address)

Best regards,

PS: I also wanted to tell you

Hello! Do you also want to eat for free while doing some household management?

I'm having an expiry-date party!

Bring any food past its sell-by date, and we can cook it together.
We shall / shall not* go to the market to forage for leftover vegetables.
Remember to check your drink stash for anything past its date!

We shall meet at (place)
Date   time
RSVP to this invite via (telephone number or email address)

Best regards,

*Delete as appropriate

PS: I also wanted to tell you

I want to impress you!

Hi, I want to show you how scholarly I am.
That's why I'm going to read you the fantastic book, **Lick It!**
You can decide which chapter and in which voice I shall read.

Of course, I shall make delicious food for the occasion, which we shall eat licking off the table.
So wear clothes that can get dirty.
You don't have to wash the dishes because we won't use crockery.

Come to (place)
Date   time
RSVP to this invite via (telephone number or email address)

Best regards,

PS: I also wanted to tell you

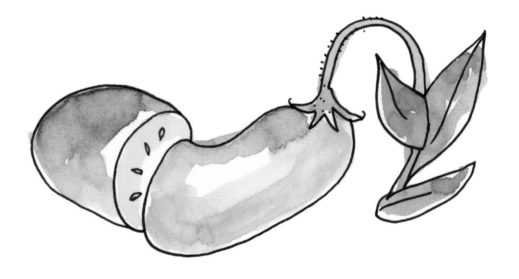

epilogue

My, there are so many books about things in the world. And now yet another book! You can spend your whole life reading only to have absorbed but a fraction of everything you can learn. Although I love to read, it's a misconception that you learn a lot while reading. To understand something, you must do things with your body, not just your head. Make something your own by experiencing it.

Have you read my book until this epilogue without doing a single challenge? Then I dare say you have withheld yourself from seventy percent of its knowledge and experience. Learning doesn't only flow through the brain. You also gain knowledge and experience through your mouth and hands and by experiencing awkwardness and challenging yourself. So if you have completed the book and there are no stains or crumbs between the pages, it's your loss. You can pass the book on to someone else.

You eat with your entire body.
When you eat, the world voyages through your body. Food is like life. It can be dirty, scruffy, strange and uncomfortable at times. But also surprising, moving, sensual, horny or heart-warming.

Whatever it is, it is your life – a life unachievable without food. I hope reading this book has helped you love food a little more. Maybe not because it tastes better now, but perhaps because it further surprises and challenges you. I also hope you have sharpened your creative thinking skills. The mind is like a kitchen tool, like a blender or a frying pan. You put something in and transform it into something similar yet very different. An omelette is an egg, but it fits much better in a sandwich. Your imagination can make everything taste different. It's like a magic wand.

A cookbook is also full of challenges, but they are called recipes.

I am incredibly grateful that I had the opportunity to make this book. It began to effervesce in me while meditating. My future self counselled, 'Make a book!' And I replied, surprised and slightly irritated, 'A book! How did you come up with that, silly?' Then the pieces fell into place while walking the Pieterpad, a 498-kilometre route the length of the Netherlands, in the summer of 2021.

I gained immense pleasure from giving the Food and Design Dive online course, where participants did small, practical challenges at home. The accessible yet challenging assignments afforded many more insights than my lectures alone. Indeed, a cookbook is also full of challenges, but they are called recipes. So why not make a book that helps you see food in a different light: by learning through the prism of doing and experimenting.

You might disagree with some parts of this book. However, the binary opposites of true and false do not interest me as much as discovering what is useful. Where can I discover an accurate angle to shine a light on something mired in darkness? Ultimately, it's not about the source of the shadow but the wellspring of light.

For more than twenty-three years, my goal has been to help people experience what the combination of food and creative thinking can do for them. Initially, I did this with catering and my restaurants and then through exhibitions, performances and installations. I established The Dutch Institute of Food & Design and teach at various academies and universities. Teaching online enables me to make food and design more accessible to a broader audience. I want to reach even more people with this book – people who once in a while place a stone among the food on their plate or wonder why they eat something and why in that particular way. This is what's great about food: it can teach us all something.

This book is just a selection of what I should like to write. I want to share many more stories about food and creative thinking. The world is full of inspiring scientists, chefs, designers, farmers and educators. They all deal with food in their own way. Was this book valuable to you, and would you like more? Let me know via **lickit@marijevogelzang.nl** or instagram: **@lickit.book**. And, of course I made many mistakes that you'll want to point out to me.

I walked the Pieterpad with Mark, who doesn't like pears but likes pear ice cream and with whom I want to walk thousands of miles more. Mark patiently wanted to listen to all the chapters. He is a theatre maker and taught me how to structure my writing so that you, the reader, would not fall asleep immediately. Thank you, dear soul mate. I should also like to thank my wonderful parents, who read along attentively and acceptingly allowed themselves to be portrayed with loving, culinary simplicity. Thank you to my dear sister Bertje, who sent me encouraging comments written on the prints in beautiful school teacher handwriting. This book is interwoven with the inspiration that bounces around me in the form of my three children: Juni, Januari and April. Thank you for your refreshingly open views. I am grateful to be your mother.

I want to thank the fantastic team that filled this book with energy.
Marleen Oud: graphic design
Priscilla de Putter: editing
JLC Coburn: English translation
Trang Ha: research, challenges
Asa, Yi-Han Yen: research assistance
Merijn Tol: mentoring and recipes
Diederik Corvers: lettertype design
Marije Vogelzang: concept, text and illustrations

Further, I should also like to thank the DOEN Foundation, the Municipality of Dordrecht and the Creative Industries Fund NL. I could not have made this book without your trust.

And finally, thank you to
Design Academy Eindhoven
The London Writer's Salon
All Food and Design Dive and Advanced Food and Design Dive participants
And all Sensitive Pirates.